JAPANESE INNS
AND HOT SPRINGS

A GUIDE TO JAPAN'S BEST
RYOKAN AND ONSEN

Akihiko Seki and Rob Goss

TUTTLE Publishing

Tokyo | Rutland, Vermont | Singapore

CONTENTS

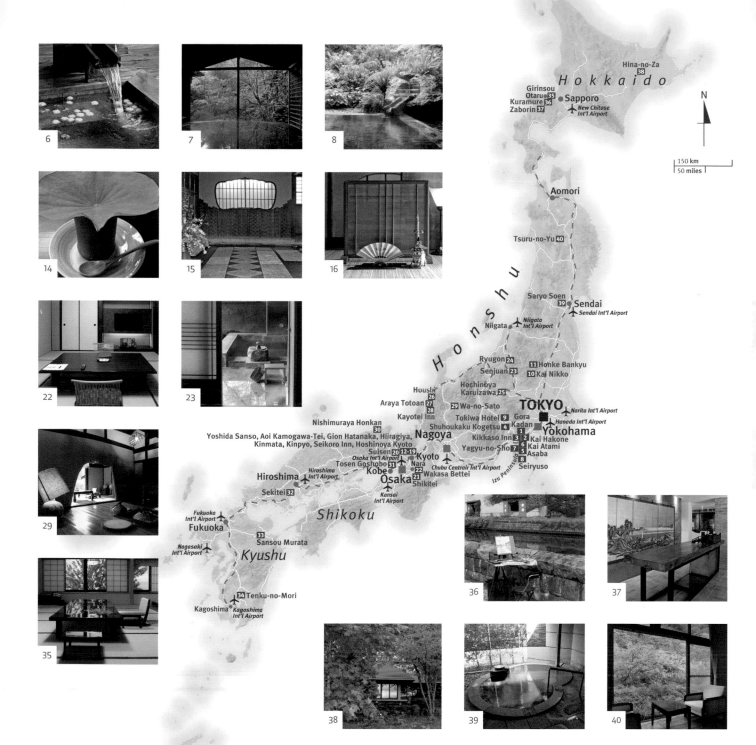

6

7

8

14

15

16

22

23

29

35

36

37

38

39

40

Hokkaido

Hina-no-Za 38

Girinsou
Otaru 35 ● Sapporo
Kuramure 36
Zaborin 37   ✈ New Chitose
Int'l Airport

N

150 km
50 miles

● Aomori

Tsuru-no-Yu 40

Honshu

Saryo Soen
39 ● Sendai
✈ Sendai Int'l Airport

Niigata ✈ Niigata
Int'l Airport

Ryugon 24
Senjuan 23   11 Honke Bankyu
                   10 Kai Nikko
Houshi 26
          Hoshinoya
          Karuizawa 25
Araya Totoan 27
              28
Kayotei Inn   29 Wa-no-Sato
                Tokiwa Hotel 9
Nishimuraya Honkan   Gora
30   Shuhoukaku Kogetsu 4 Kadan **TOKYO** ✈ Narita Int'l Airport
                                        1
Yoshida Sanso, Aoi Kamogawa-Tei, Gion Hatanaka, Hiiragiya,   ● Yokohama ✈ Haneda Int'l Airport
Kinmata, Kinpyo, Seikoro Inn, Hoshinoya Kyoto   Kikkaso Inn 3 1 2 Kai Hakone
Suisen 20 12-19 **Kyoto** **Nagoya** Yagyu-no-Sho 6 5 Kai Atami
✈ Osaka Int'l Airport   Nara   7 Asaba
Tosen Goshobo 31   22   8
Kobe   Chubu Centrair Int'l Airport ✈ Seiryuso
Osaka   21 Wakasa Bettei
Hiroshima   Shikitei   *Izu Peninsula*
Int'l Airport ✈
Hiroshima
Sekitei 32

Shikoku

Fukuoka
Int'l Airport ✈
Fukuoka 33
              Sansou Murata
Nagasaki
Int'l Airport ✈
Kyushu

34 Tenku-no-Mori
Kagoshima ● Kagoshima
             Int'l Airport ✈

THE RYOKAN EXPERIENCE

Above An elegant starter course at Hoshinoya Karuizawa (see pages 140–143). Multi-course *kaiseki* meals are an integral part of the ryokan experience and many ryokan pride themselves on providing meals that are better than what you get in an expensive Michelin-starred restaurant. Of course the room rates reflect this, but keep in mind that half or more of what you are paying for is the food.

Browsing through the ryokan brochures at a Japanese travel agency reveals much about the variation and intricacies of the ryokan. Some ryokan specialize in food, at others the baths are the star, while with a few the history and traditions are the main appeal, but in most cases it's the combination of factors that makes a ryokan special. Take somewhere like Hoshinoya Kyoto, a contemporary ryokan, where you'll find Michelin-starred cuisine coupled with a blend of European and Japanese design sensibilities. At the historic Hiiragiya in Kyoto, the lore of the ryokan itself combines with impeccable hospitality and the finest of traditional *kaiseki* cuisine.

One thing that unites all great ryokan, of course, is the food. The seasonal produce, regional specialties, and presentation will vary from ryokan to ryokan, but dinner usually follows the multi-course *kaiseki* template with a set succession of anywhere between seven or eight to a dozen or so courses. The culinary procession begins with a small, often single bite appetizer course—called *sakizuke*—designed to whet the appetite before the second course, the *hassun*, which appears with a larger selection of small dishes that will almost always include a fish of some

kind and several other ornately presented seasonal morsels.

Next typically comes the *mukozuke*, a selection of three or four types of sashimi; perhaps a few slices of sea bream and some succulent small shrimp or scallop hearts. The season and the region will determine the selection, but being sashimi, all will of course be raw for dipping in a little wasabi and soy sauce. Next up comes the simmered *takiawase* dish, which could be any combination of vegetables or tofu with meat or seafood, and then the *futamono* dish—a light soup. After that will likely be a flame-broiled *yakimono* dish, which more often than not is seafood, before a vinegared *suzakana* dish that refreshes the palate ahead of the main dish (although several other small courses may also follow first), which could be anything from a hotpot of local seafood to a *teppan* grilled dish featuring prime regional beef or highly prized abalone.

Near the end of the meal, just when you are beginning to wonder if you can physically manage to eat anything else, will come the *gohan* (rice; often including vegetables or seafood), *konomono* (pickles) and *tomewan* (miso soup) courses, and to round things off the *mizumono* (dessert), which could be as simple as sliced fruit or

The *okami* or "house mother" at the Yoshida Sanso (see pages 76–81) and her daughter. Personal attention and service by experienced *okami* are a key part of the ryokan experience. They literally take care of you as your mother would—including serving lavish meals in your room.

as tempting as a green tea crème brûlée. As you roll away from the dinner table, just remember that in less than twelve hours' time you will be back at the table working your way through a multi-course breakfast.

It's for this reason that most high-quality ryokan don't offer no-meal stays; after all, they employ some of the country's best chefs, sometimes serving only several groups a night in the smallest of ryokan, so they simply wouldn't be able to survive on room-only customers. Even if they did offer a no-meal option, given that it's common to only stay a single night at a ryokan, to go without the food would be to miss out on a crucial element of the experience—it's more than worth the splurge.

Then, of course, there are the baths. From working on this book I've learned that with so many subtle and not so subtle variations between ryokan, there really isn't a typical ryokan per se. It is common for ryokan to offer a mixture of bathing options, from small private in-room baths to a selection of large communal bathing areas that might feature an outdoor bath accented by rocks or with views into nature, and indoor wooden baths that might give off the gentle scent of cypress or be infused with citrus. Given that many ryokan are in geothermically active

Right Tosen Goshobo (see pages 164–167). Volcanic hot-spring bathing with water direct from the ground is another vital feature of the high-quality ryokan in this book.

regions, it's common too for the bath waters to come straight from natural hot-spring sources deep beneath the ryokan, at a naturally piping hot, muscle-relaxing 40 or so degrees Celsius (104 degrees Farenheit) that makes a hot-spring soak one of Japan's most treasured treats. One that's said to be healthy, too, with the mineral-rich waters attributed with alleviating ailments as diverse as arthritis and piles.

With the design of a ryokan there are also certain unifying elements, although as this book hopefully demonstrates, there is great variety, too. Rooms in traditional ryokan frequently feature tatami mat flooring and at night futon are laid out on the floor. In one part of the room you'll find an alcove, called a *tokonoma*, where a pictorial or calligraphic scroll will be hung, perhaps alongside a flower arrangement. The center of the room will have a low table, where etiquette dictates that the most important guest sits with his or her back to the *tokonoma*. There'll be sliding screen doors, too, and laid out on arrival will be your cotton *yukata* gown, which you can change into for the duration of your stay, allowing you to shed your real-world clothes and immerse yourself in the past.

Above Many ryokan have rustic designs or even employ old farmhouse buildings like Wa-no-Sato (pages 156–159), located in Gifu Prefecture.

Right All ryokan place a high value on comfort, which includes the sleeping arrangements. Typically this means a comfortable futon bed laid out each night on a soft tatami floor, but some ryokan, like Seiryuso (see pages 58-61) also feature Western-style beds.

Above Ryokan rooms are designed for relaxation, which often means contemplation of a beautifully designed Japanese garden, such as this one at Asaba (pages 40–45).

A TRADITION OF FINE HOSPITALITY

As anyone who has stayed at a ryokan will tell you, the experience is more than a window to classic Japan, it affords an opportunity to immerse yourself in tradition; to experience old Japan as the Japanese have done for generations—in a way that is unadulterated, unhurried, and undoubtedly unforgettable.

Like so much of Japan's richly woven cultural tapestry, the ryokan has a long and winding history that has seen it develop from humble beginnings to today's pampering retreat. Delve into the ryokan's roots and you'll be reaching back to the Nara period (710–784), a time when the political, social and religious structures of classical Japanese civilization were taking shape. It was then that simple but free rest houses for travelers called *fuseya* first appeared. They were run by Buddhist monks to help keep travelers from the perils of the road.

In the Heian era (794–1191), a rise in the popularity of pilgrimages among the elite classes saw a twist on *fuseya* arise, with feudal manors and temples opening themselves to pilgrims. It's hard to know just how spartan the latter—called *shukubo*—would have been back then, but the modern-day version of temple accommodation is a fascinating experience for pilgrims and tourists alike. In Koya-san, the mountain-top town home to the Shingon sect of Buddhism, almost half of the one hundred or so temples and monasteries that hug the mountain provide almost ryokan-like *shukubo*, with modest tatami-mat rooms but exquisite vegetarian *shojin-ryori* cuisine and opportunities to experience temple life by attending morning prayers and meditation.

It's difficult to entirely separate *shukubo* from ryokan—many current ryokan, for example, were once *shukubo*. But as temple lodgings developed on major travel routes, along with the development of roads, bridges, and small towns, so did accommodation for non-pilgrims. Initially, this took the form of simple lodgings called *kichin-yado*, where guests received no meals but were able to seek shelter from the elements. Guests were charged not for their

Above Personal service at a ryokan not only means lavish ten-course meals in your room but occasionally the chef may even serve you personally, as shown here at Suisen (pages 116–121). **Opposite** Most of the ryokan in this book (except for those in the historic districts of Kyoto and Nara) are located in the countryside in a gorgeous setting, like Yagyu-no-Sho (pages 52–57).

This modern hot-spring pool at
Gora Kadan (see pages 20-25) is carved
from a block of solid granite.

rooms here, but for the wood they would use to cook and keep warm with. By the time of the Edo era (1603–1868), a developing economy and increased internal trade saw more travel, and the appearance of accommodation called *hatago*, offering merchants and other travelers a more comprehensive version of *kichin-yado*, with meals provided and accommodation fees charged.

At this time, with the Tokugawa shogunate strictly keeping provincial lords in check, a high-end version of *hatago* also came in to being, and besides being another stepping stone toward today's ryokan, its own roots reveal much about the politics of the Edo era. So the shogunate could keep a close eye on them, *daimyo* (feudal lords) were obliged to alternate annually between living in their own regions and living in the capital Edo (now called Tokyo). This saw the rise of *honjin* lodgings for the *daimyo* on common travel routes, as well as less fancy lodgings for their staff, but even with these

and *hatago* in place another development was needed before the ryokan became what it is today—widespread travel for leisure.

From the Meiji Restoration in 1868, when military rule with its harsh travel restrictions was abolished, travel and sightseeing as a pastime began to grow in popularity, initially among the wealthy, then spreading to a broad spectrum of society from the end of the Second World War onwards. As a result, ryokan—the kanji characters for which literally translate to something like "travel lodgings"—sprang up all over Japan, particularly in popular tourist destinations and in areas blessed with natural hot springs, offering a relaxing combination of traditional peace and quiet, hospitality, fine cuisine, and (in many cases) hot-spring bathing. The ryokan offers pampering, but also an opportunity for Japanese living increasingly hectic, modern lives to slow down; to embrace and celebrate their traditions; to feel Japanese.

The opportunity to experience a traditional Japanese home interior first-hand is one of the great joys of staying at a ryokan. Shown here is an elegant room at Yoshida Sanso (see pages 76–81).

A GUIDE TO RYOKAN ETIQUETTE

Entire books have been written on Japanese business etiquette and social manners. In the most part, the intricacies don't apply to tourists—just use universal good manners and you'll be fine—but there are some particular rules for the ryokan that you should do your best to follow.

When to Remove Your Shoes

In the majority of ryokan, you take off your shoes in the entrance area before stepping into the ryokan, store them in the lockers or on the shoe shelves available, and then change into slippers to be worn around the communal areas of the ryokan. When you get to your room, you then remove your slippers at the room's *genkan* (the small entrance area), going barefoot or in socks on the tatami mats. There can be variations, of course—some ryokan, for example, allow shoes throughout the communal areas, but you then take these off at your *genkan*—which can make things a little confusing. A simple guideline is to never step on tatami with shoes or slippers on and, wherever else, look out for slippers. If slippers are laid out, it's a good bet you should be using them.

Luggage

As well as removing your shoes at the entrance, at most ryokan this is also where staff will collect your luggage from you. If you end up carrying your own luggage to your room, lift it up if you can, so that the wheels don't bring in dirt from outside or damage the flooring. In your room, don't keep the luggage on the tatami or in the *tokonoma*. There will be closets or other areas to leave it.

Right At Asaba (pages 40–45), you are personally greeted by the *okami* who will look after you during your stay. Remember to remove your shoes at the entrance! (She will store them for you.)

Opposite page Kinmata (pages 96–99). Your luggage will be brought to your room. Be very careful not to damage the tatami mats, paper screens and furniture in the room or public areas. If anything is damaged, you might be asked to pay for the cost of repairing or replacing the items.

Right The first course of a meal at Kinmata (pages 96–99). Breakfast and dinner at a ryokan are both lavish affairs requiring many hours of preparation by the kitchen. You will be asked to confirm your preferred meal times in advance. Be punctual to avoid disrupting the ryokan's carefully choreographed schedule.

Bath Time

First up, change into the cotton *yukata* gown left for you in your room before going to the bathhouse (you can wear this throughout your stay), and take one of the room towels with you as not all ryokan have towels in the bathhouse. Once there, get naked, leaving your *yukata* and anything else in one of the wicker baskets or lockers in the changing room next to the actual bath room. Unless you are at a mixed-gender bath (although many of these are nude only, too) the only thing allowed in the bath is you—no bathing shorts, towels, or anything else to protect your modesty.

Next, the most important thing is to wash before getting in the bath. As a foreigner, you can be forgiven for many faux pas in Japan, but polluting a communal bath with soap or dirt is one cardinal sin that nobody gets away with. Before getting in the bath for a long, hot soak, take a seat on one of the little stools by the low showers and wash and fully rinse (making sure to rinse off any soap and bubbles from the stool too) before heading for the bath. Enter the bath gently, as it's rude to disturb the water too much, and then relax.

Tipping

Basically speaking: no. Whether at a taxi, restaurant, hotel or anywhere else, tipping is very rarely done in Japan. In almost all situations, simply trying to tip someone would cause embarrassment. That said, with very high-end ryokan there is an old custom (seldom followed nowadays) of offering a gratuity for staff who were particularly helpful. This is done by slipping a little cash (¥2,000 to ¥3,000) into an envelope and discreetly handing it over. Again, you aren't expected to do this (quite the opposite), and you may be politely refused. If you want to leave something to say thank you for a great stay, give the staff a box of cookies or something similar when you check out. Really, though, a genuine thank you and smile is more than enough.

Noise Levels

You don't have to whisper or walk around like you are on eggshells, but the peace and quiet is something that makes ryokan so special. In common areas especially, a little common sense will go a long way when it comes to noise and, if you are traveling with kids, make sure they aren't running amok.

Meals

Ingredients are ordered to meet the day's demand, so don't make any last-minute menu requests as the ryokan might not be able to accommodate them. If you have special dietary requirements, let the ryokan know before you arrive. Be aware that dinner timings tend not to be flexible, beyond perhaps the choice of dinner at 6:30 or 7pm, as the chefs will cook all the intricate dishes at one time on a tight schedule, to be served at once. When you've set the time, you need to stick to it. Ryokan won't hold a meal for you, as they won't want to serve food that isn't at its freshest.

Left Hiiragaya (pages 90–95). Paper *shoji* screens are exquisitely beautiful but also extremely fragile. Please be careful when opening them.

GORA KADAN HAKONE

With its collection of hot-spring baths, spa treatments, and timeless ryokan style, this former Imperial villa in the mountains of Hakone offers one of the most luxurious weekend escapes from Tokyo.

Above A cobbled pathway leads to the main entrance.
Below A small garden feature (for purification purposes) that wouldn't look out of place at the entrance to the inner grounds of a shrine.

Located on the grounds of the former summer villa of a member of the Imperial Family—in the village of Gora, midway through the classic sightseeing route around the Hakone area—the Gora Kadan initially opened as a ryokan in 1952, undergoing a major modernizing renovation in 1989 that has given the ryokan its current combination of traditional and contemporary styles.

The appreciation of nature is an important part of the experience at many of the best ryokan—as well as in traditional Japanese culture in general—and at the Gora Kadan opportunities to connect with nature abound. The setting, in the northern part of Fuji-Hakone-Izu National Park, means guests are treated to lush mountain views, while in spots like the moon-viewing deck they can watch bamboo sway and listen to the sound of a small stream, while taking in star-studded skies—weather permitting of course.

The guest rooms build on this connection with nature. Rooms in the Annex Suites feature private open-air baths that overlook the Gora Kadan's historic landscaped garden; other suite rooms boast open-air rock, stone, or wooden baths that look out into nature. Even the "standard" rooms have their own aromatic indoor wooden baths that draw on natural hot-spring wells, as well as their own small private gardens. And regardless of the class

Above left One of the outdoor communal baths. Gora Kadan's water, which feeds the communal and in-room baths, is a mineral-rich source from deep under Hakone. One of its attributes is to leave one's skin feeling soft and smooth.

Above right A room with a view. Many of the non-standard rooms come with facilities such as outdoor baths, wood decking with panoramic or semi-panoramic views, and a sense of being within nature.

Right One of the outdoor guest room baths. With the soothing heat of the water, soaking up to your chin in one of these feels just as good as a full-body massage.

of room, each features a smart mix of traditional design elements such as tatami matting, sliding paper screen doors and lightly toned woods that give both a freshness and a feeling of spaciousness.

Since 1981, Gora Kadan has been a member of the Relais & Chateaux association of independently owned luxury hotels and restaurants, and in 2002 it was awarded the organization's prestigious Welcome Trophy in recognition of high customer satisfaction and high standards of service. It's not hard to see why. As well as in-room baths, there are two large communal baths that draw on piping hot mineral-rich spring water, soothing and relaxing in the midst of nature. The nightly *kaiseki* is an artistic multi-course treat served in-room by kimono-clad staff and employing seafood sourced fresh from the local waters of Suruga Gulf and Sagami Bay as well as other fine produce brought in from around Japan. Beyond the normal facilities one finds at a ryokan, Gora Kadan also incorporates a covered swimming pool, a jacuzzi, and a gym, not to mention a spa that offers a range of aesthetic treatments such as full-body massages, facials and aromatherapy.

The location is terrific, too. Guests can easily access tourist attractions such as the Hakone Open Air Museum (home to a

Above In-room baths come in a variety of styles, like this aromatic cedar tub.
Left Design-wise, the spa looks extremely traditional, but the massages and other treatments available there have an eclectic feel, with shiatsu, acupuncture, detox, stone therapy, and more on the menu.

Below Relaxation at the Gora Kadan goes beyond a soak in the bath and a massage. You could lounge by the pool all day if you wanted, or do something very rare at a ryokan—use it to get some exercise.

Right After a traditional ryokan breakfast, you very often don't need lunch. If you aren't used to it, rice, fish, pickles, soup (and more) can be quite a challenging start to the day. But, it invites you to take your time, and a slow breakfast sets one up for a relaxing day ahead.

large Picasso collection as well as many outdoor art installations), the steaming volcanic landscape of the Owakudani valley, and Lake Ashi with its postcard-perfect view of Mount Fuji. See page 33 for further information on Hakone's attractions.

Gora Kadan 強羅花壇
Address: 1300 Gora, Hakone, Ashigarashimo, Kanagawa 250-0408
Telephone: 0460-82-3331
Website: www.gorakadan.com
Email: info@gorakadan.com
Number of rooms: 38
Room rate: ¥¥¥¥

KAI HAKONE HAKONE

The KAI's distinctive blend of local customs and refined tradition with sleek contemporary touches really comes to the fore at the KAI Hakone's Yosegi-no-Ma room, which is designed using local crafts as a key motif.

Situated on the banks of a mountain river, a short taxi ride from Hakone-Yumoto Station in the heart of the Hakone area, KAI Hakone is a traditional ryokan tweaked to satisfy modern-day guests.

Step inside and you will be met by staff dressed in black rather than in kimono. In place of green tea comes a welcome glass of sparkling wine served in a cavernous lobby, with natural wood flooring and furnishings and floor-to-ceiling windows that give panoramic views of greenery.

From the lobby, a corridor of bamboo leads to the guest rooms, which are spread over four floors and all overlook the river. Floors one to three have twenty-three Japanese-style rooms that feature low sofas and beds and offer an open space that combines a tatami-matted sitting area and wood-floored bedroom, plus wide windows for taking in the sights and sounds of nature outside. On the fourth floor are eight Western-style rooms, with carpeting and contemporary, unfussy interiors.

However, if you want a room that says Hakone like no other, book the KAI's Yosegi-no-Ma, which has been decorated using a distinctive local craft called *yosegi* marquetry, a type of woodworking that uses different colors and tones of wood to give a mosaic-like appearance. In Hakone's souvenir stores, you see everything from *yosegi* boxes and trays to cups and cupboards, and the Yosegi-no-Ma room has gone all out to incorporate these and *yosegi*-patterned furnishings in its design to very striking effect. Taking the theme a step further, every night in the lobby guests can make their own *yosegi* coasters; a fun activity and resulting in a souvenir that will be a real conversation-starter.

Like the Yosegi-no-Ma room, dinner is an elaborate affair. The ten-course *kaiseki* might start with an appetizer like salmon roe with sea urchin, before the *hassun* plate of delicacies, which, depending on the season, could include morsels such as steamed chicken with butterbur sprout miso, sea urchin mixed with agar, or thinly sliced potato dressed in flying fish roe. A standout dish here is the chef's special Meiji *gyu no nabe* hot pot, which features

One of the KAI Hakone's signatures—a *nabe* (which roughly translates as a hot pot) of high-grade beef cooked in a miso-based sauce.

succulent chunks of steak cooked in a miso-based sauce.

Hakone is renowned in Japan for its abundance of natural hot springs—there are twenty in the area, and bathing is a key part of any ryokan stay here. Drawing on water from the Hakone Yumoto hot spring, the KAI's two semi open-air communal baths (one for men, one for women) feature large "infinity" bathtubs with vast open windows that frame the lush riverside scenery.

Hakone is also renowned as one of the most popular weekend retreats from Tokyo, in part because of its ryokan and baths, but also because it's a fun area to explore. Using Hakone-Yumoto Station as a starting point, and going through a succession of different forms of transportation (from switchback railway to cable car and ropeway), guests at the KAI can easily head up into the mountains to see sights like the Hakone Open Air Museum, the historic Fujiya Hotel (see page 32), the mountain village of Gora, the

Balancing out the hearty flavor of the Meiji *nabe* (above), the meals also include the finesse of intricate dishes like these. Striking to look at yet sublime on the palette.

Left The communal baths are semi open-air and ion-rich, with a gentle coolness coming from the woods and the river that runs alongside the KAI. The way the opening in the building frames nature is a classic concept, albeit on a grand scale here.

steaming volcanic valley of Owakudani, and then drop down to the picturesque Lake Ashi—a route that also offers up various glimpses of Mount Fuji.

Hoshino Resorts KAI Hakone 界 箱根
Address: 230 Yumoto-chaya, Hakone-machi, Ashigarashimo, Kanagawa 250-0312
Telephone: 050-3786-1144
Website: www.hoshinoresorts.com/en/resortsandhotels/kai/hakone
Email: hakone@kai-ryokan.jp
Number of rooms: 32
Room rate: ¥¥

Above and right There's always something special about a little sake at a ryokan. You could take it with natural views on one of the terraces (right) or, if you are in the Yosegi-no-Ma room (above), which is designed on *yosegi* marquetry themes (a Hakone craft), while enjoying the striking woodwork.

KIKKASO INN HAKONE

With just three rooms, a night at the Kikkaso is both intimate and tranquil. It's a rare opportunity to have a former Imperial villa almost all to oneself, picturesque garden included.

History. The Fujiya Hotel in Hakone, one of Japan's classic Western-style hotels, is steeped in it. Since opening in 1878, it has functioned as a luxury retreat for royalty and the stars, from Japan's own Imperial Family to the likes of Charlie Chaplin, Helen Keller, and John Lennon. Explore the buildings and grounds and the past immerses you. Old photographs of famous guests adorn many of the hallway walls, there are art deco interiors, aging woods, and stairs that creak as you climb them. But that's not all. The Fujiya contains one of Hakone's best kept secrets, the Kikkaso Inn.

Built in 1895 as a summer villa for the Emperor and Empress Meiji, and used by various members of the Imperial Family into the 1940s (when the Fujiya took control of it), the Kikkaso oozes old charm. Visit the tatami-mat dining area, where you can take a multi-dish *kaiseki* dinner if you don't opt for the highly rated French cuisine at the Fujiya, and you'll be eating in what was once the Emperor's bedroom. Look at the pillars of Japanese cypress here and you will still see some of the iron rings that would have held up the Imperial mosquito nets, as well as iron light fittings bearing the Imperial chrysanthemum crest.

It's the staff that ultimately make a good ryokan stay. The concept of *omotenashi*—roughly meaning hospitality but with a deeper nuance of understanding and anticipating a guest's needs— is sometimes over-hyped nowadays and when done badly lacks flexibility, but at the best ryokan, it's the key to the experience. Generations of service means places like the Kikkaso get *omotenashi* just right every time.

The Imperial adventure continues outside, where Kikkaso guests have exclusive access to the Imperial Family's once-private stroll garden. Like the Kikkaso, which is the smallest of the former Imperial villas in Japan, the garden is an intimate affair, with a mossy pathway leading up to a small "hill" that has a view over the villa, and where a carp-filled pond is accented by a vivid vermilion bridge. Like the Meiji and Showa emperors before them, it's very likely guests will enjoy their stroll in complete peace and quiet—there are, after all, only three guest rooms at the Kikkaso, all following the classic ryokan formula of tatami flooring, paper screen doors and, at night, futon arranged on the floor for sleeping.

If the historic charm of the Kikkaso and the glamorous atmosphere of the Fujiya Hotel were not enough, the surrounding location also has much to recommend it. Hakone has long been a popular overnight retreat for generations of Tokyoites, because of its easy access (one hour forty minutes from Shinjuku Station in Tokyo to Hakone by the Romancecar express train), its proximity to Mount Fuji, natural hot-spring baths, and other natural attractions. The Kikkaso is conveniently situated for easy access to many local areas of interest.

Using the trundling Tozan railway, the two-carriage switchback service that many guests take from Hakone-Yumoto Station to Miyanoshita Station, which serves the Fujiya, you can go higher and deeper into the Hakone area. Two stops up the line, at Chokoku-no-Mori Station, is the Hakone Open-air Art Museum which has a sprawling collection of outdoor sculptures, as well as a large indoor Picasso collection. One stop on, at the end of the line, comes the town of Gora, from where a funicular train runs to Mount Soun. After taking in the views here, you can take a cable car over the volcanic valley of Owakudani—a barren range dotted with bubbling

hot-spring pools and steaming sulfur vents. The cable car journey ends at the attractive Lake Ashi, which offers spectacular views of Mount Fuji when the weather is clear.

Fujiya Hotel, Kikkaso Inn 菊華荘
Address: 359 Miyanoshita, Hakone-machi, Ashigarashimo-gun, Kanagawa, Japan 250-0404
Telephone: 0460-82-2211
Website: www.fujiyahotel.jp
Email: info@fujiyahotel.jp
Number of rooms: 3
Room rate: ¥¥¥

Above Guests at the Kikkaso have the option of a traditional *kaiseki* course featuring dishes like this, but can also dine on French cuisine at the main Fujiya Hotel.

Top right The three guest rooms at the Fujiya are relatively modest, but fully traditional. That, of course, includes the low table in the main room being moved at night and futon being prepared on the floor, so guests can fall asleep to the gentle scent of tatami.

Right The garden is one of the loveliest features of the Kikkaso, especially with the accent given by the striking vermilion bridge.

About as close to a stay in the shadow of Mount Fuji as you can find, the Kogetsu gives mesmerizing views of Japan's tallest and most iconic peak from its lakeside berth.

Left The entrance to the hot-spring baths. The swirly looking character is one ryokan and hot-spring fans will see often. It's the phonetic hiragana character for "yu", meaning hot water, but here signifying the hot baths.

Mount Fuji, Japan's highest and most iconic peak, has inspired generations of Japanese, from artists like Hokusai and his famed woodblock prints to the haiku master Matsuo Basho. The mountain, snow-capped for much of the year, is visible as far afield as Tokyo, and has been claimed as sacred by Shinto and Buddhism. Mount Fuji has shaped Japanese culture like no other natural monument. And whether seen for the first time or the hundredth, its beauty always captivates.

Though it can be seen from far and wide, few places in Japan offer better views of Fuji-san—as the Japanese call it—than Lake Kawaguchi, sixty-two miles (one hundred kilometers) west of Tokyo in Yamanashi Prefecture's Five Lakes area. And few places at Lake Kawaguchi boast

better views of Fuji than the Kogetsu ryokan on the lake's northern shoreline. From the Kogetsu's two communal outdoor hot-spring baths, Fuji appears across the lake in all its symmetrical magnificence. On some winter mornings, when the light is just right, its surface appears reddish, and on some nights, when the moonlight deems it fit, it appears to float on the lake—phenomena known as *akafuji* (red Fuji) and *kurofuji* (black Fuji), respectively.

Like the baths, all the rooms come with Fuji views; some of the non-standard rooms have their own wood-decked terraces where guests can relax in loungers or soothe their feet in private footbaths while taking in the scenery; others have private open-air baths too. Looking inside, all are bright and airy, with light tatami, walls, and wood, and either futon or

simple Western-style beds. Most guests will have dinner served in their room (though large groups can have their own dining rooms), and at the Kogetsu—like most ryokan—that means an elaborate *kaiseki* affair featuring mostly local, seasonal produce turned into dishes such as richly fragrant *matsutake* mushroom soup and a *shabu shabu* hot pot featuring pork from pigs that have been reared on Koshu wine.

What makes Lake Kawaguchi great for a weekend away from Tokyo—besides the scenery, the ryokan, and the hot-spring baths—is the variety of things to do here. It's an easy drive from Kawaguchiko to the amusement park Fuji-Q Highland, which has a terror-inducing selection of white-knuckle rides. In the lake area itself is the Itchiku

Left The Kogetsu's baths have Fuji views. If the conditions are right, some mornings you can get a glimpse of *akafuji* (when Fuji takes on a red hue) or of an evening *kurofuji* (when the mountain appears to float in the moonlight).

Above The choice of serving dish is just as important as the arrangement of the food itself. During the dinner, you are invited to enjoy not just taste, but to appreciate design.

Left A member of staff serves a welcome drink shortly after arriving at the guestroom. As well as being the first opportunity to unwind after traveling, the welcome drink service is also the first opportunity to get to know the staff member who (very likely) will be serving and looking after you throughout your stay.

Kubota Art Museum, which houses decorative tie-dyed kimono and other fabrics. Around the lake, there are also herb gardens and, in spring, vast fields of pink moss phlox that create a stark contrast to Fuji. The lake area is also close to trails that lead to Fuji's peak, when the summer climbing season opens and thousands of hikers make the slow trek up to 12,388 feet (3,776 meters) in the hope of seeing the sunrise from Japan's highest point. More than anything, there's just something special about being so close to Fuji, soaking outside in a hot bath as the sun sets, or whiling away an afternoon on the decking taking in the views.

The *rotemburo* (outdoor bath) comes with lovely lake views, although if you stand up for long you run the risk of flashing any passing boats.

Shuhoukaku Kogetsu 湖月
Address: 2312 Kawaguchi, Fuji Kawaguchiko, Minami-tsuru-gun, Yamanashi 401-0304
Telephone: 0555-76-8888
Website: www.kogetu.com
Email: info@kogetu.com
Number of rooms: 45
Room rate: ¥¥¥

Left With a shoreline just short of twelve miles (twenty kilometers) long, Lake Kawaguchi is the second-largest of the Fuji Five Lakes. As well as options to take to the water in tour boats or swan-shaped pedalos, there are also pretty walking trails around the lake and a good range of other attractions.

Below The guest rooms have a wonderful simplicity in design, allowing the understated traditional elements to shine.

This tipple might look like sake, but it's actually wine. Japan is far from being a major winemaker, but within Japan, Yamanashi is known for its wines.

The Asaba is a standout in so many ways. Not only has it been in the same family since the fifteenth century, it even has its own outdoor Noh stage, where performances take place several times a year.

Ever since the monk Kobo Daishi (aka Kukai)—the founder of Shingon Buddhism—visited what is now the town of Shuzenji in the early 800s and discovered the area's natural hot-spring source before then establishing the temple that gave its name to the town, Shuzenji has been synonymous with both Buddhism and bathing. With Shuzenji Temple at its heart, the town flourished as a regional center for Shingon Buddhism for nearly five hundred years. Then came a couple of hundred years of gradual decline under the Rinzai sect of Buddhism during the Kamakura era (1185–1333), when Japan was ruled from Kamakura by the Minamoto clan, before the temple was adopted by Soto Buddhism in the late 1400s. Since then, the temple has enjoyed centuries of prominence, despite going

Above Shuzenji is a pretty hot-spring town. The river running through it is transformed by rusts and yellows in autumn, but it's a pleasant place to stroll any time of year, and it's close to the Asaba. You could also walk to historic sites like Shuzenji Temple, try the outdoor footbath on the river or just take in the sights with one of the matcha ice creams you can find around here.

through the typical pattern of destruction and rebuild that has affected so many of Japan's fire-prone historic structures.

It was with the onset of Shuzenji's Soto years that the town saw the creation of its now famed ryokan, the Asaba, established by the Asaba family in 1489 (and still run by them today). Asaba began as temple lodgings but eventually morphed into an exclusive retreat during the Meiji era (1868–1912)—complete with an outdoor Noh stage visible from guest rooms. Now it is one of a select few properties in Japan with membership of the Relais & Chateaux association of independently owned luxury hotels and restaurants.

The room views, over a large pond toward the Noh stage and a wooded backdrop that turns red and yellow in the fall, are as alluring as the interiors. The

Left There are plenty of quiet spots at the Asaba where guests can enjoy the ryokan's calm and tranquility.

Below Heading for the Noh stage by boat. It's quite an entrance and an even more unforgettable performance. Noh is staged here a number of times a year, and once announced Asaba books out quickly. If you manage to get a reservation on a performance night, you'll be able to watch the show looking down on the stage from the comfort of your own room—better than any royal box.

rooms are classically appointed with tatami matting, sliding doors and other traditional touches, and the common areas are bright and spacious, featuring light woods, tatami-matted or carpeted hallways, and wide windows that open out onto the pond.

For relaxation, there are rocky outdoor hot-spring baths infused with the sweet scent of *yuzu* citrus, or a contemporary white-walled lounge serving cocktails and other drinks. There's also an on-site European-inspired spa with a variety of body and facial treatments. And then there's the food. Served in-room, the dinner at the Asaba is a supreme example of multi-course *kaiseki* cuisine incorporating seasonal produce and local specialties, weaving together platters of sashimi and in-season appetizers, with perhaps some river crab or conger eel

Above and above right The bathing options include indoor and outdoor communal baths. Both have *yuzu* citrus floating in them, which gives an intense, yet calming aroma while soaking in the piping hot waters.

Opposite page, above left As is the case with the communal areas, the guest room's use of light woods and tatami gives them a refreshing brightness. The Asaba is a very historic property but certainly doesn't feel like a museum.

Left Like the dinner, breakfast is a classic Japanese affair, featuring in-season grilled fish, rice, miso soup, egg, and a variety of small vegetable dishes and pickles. As with most ryokan, both meals come as part of the accommodation package and are served in the guest room.

stuffed with sticky rice, and maybe a hearty hot pot featuring local boar.

From the Asaba, it's an easy walk to take in the main sights of Shuzenji, crossing the distinctive red Kaede Bridge for a stroll through a small bamboo grove before following the river that cuts through the town to the Tokku-no-Yu footbath on the rocky riverbank—the hot spring that Kobo Daishi is said to have discovered and pronounced as holy on his first visit to the area—and on to the nearby Shuzenji Temple. By the standards of many of Japan's leading temples and shrines, Shuzenji is quite modest (there's none of the gilding of Kinkakuji Temple in Kyoto nor the intricate carvings of Toshogu Shrine in Nikko), but like the town—and like the Asaba—there's a calming peace and quiet in the grounds.

Asaba あさば

Address: 3450-1 Shuzenji, Izu, Shizuoka
410-2416
Telephone: 0558-72-7000
Website: www.asaba-ryokan.com/en
Email: asaba@izu.co.jp
Number of rooms: 17
Room rate: ¥¥¥¥

Top right Served in-room on a mix of regal lacquerware and fine ceramics, the multi-course *kaiseki* draws on local produce, which might include river fish or even wild boar depending on the time of year. This being Shizuoka, there will also be excellent seafood on the menu.

Right Asaba as night falls. The pond adds to both the beauty and the tranquility of the ryokan, and by day it isn't uncommon to be able to watch kingfishers flitting around it.

With a pair of aromatic outdoor baths overlooking the ocean and a hillside building that oozes old charm, KAI Atami shines in an area with a rich tradition of ryokan hospitality.

Left Cobblestones and bamboo lead to the entrance, the gentle lights at the end of the path draw you in.
Opposite page, top right It isn't just Kyoto that has a long geisha heritage. Tokyo, of course, does too. And so does Atami. Celebrating that, a local geisha performs nightly after dinner at KAI Atami, giving guests the opportunity to enjoy traditional music and dance, but also take part in fun games like fan-tossing.

Whether KAI or Hoshinoya, dinner at any Hoshino Resort property is a special experience. The *kaiseki* here draws a lot on the area's highly regarded seafood and is put together with traditional aplomb.

The resort town of Atami, looking out over Sagami Bay on the picturesque Izu-Hanto Peninsula, has long been a holiday destination synonymous with hot-spring bathing and traditional accommodation. For generations, Tokyoites in particular have been making the sixty-two–mile (hundred-kilometer) jaunt west, leaving the rigors of the city behind to relax in the mineral-rich hot-spring waters that feed Atami's numerous ryokan and unwind in timeless retreats like the KAI Atami ryokan.

Now part of Hoshino Resorts' KAI range, in many respects the 160-year-old KAI Atami is the quintessential ryokan. After leaving your shoes at the entranceway and then slipping into your cotton *yukata* gown, you become part of a hushed world where the pace of life slows to allow contemplation and calm; and where the senses can hone in on the finest of details—the mellow aroma of green tea, the sweet scent of tatami, the sound of waves in the distance.

The building, though home to just sixteen guest rooms, is an intriguing maze of hallways and stairways spread out on a hillside overlooking the bay, close enough to the ocean to hear waves lapping as you fall asleep at night, yet high enough up the hill to take in broad ocean views from the guest rooms and from the large open-air communal cedar baths. Likewise, the open-air lounge halfway up the hillside, where guests can unwind with complimentary drinks, provides not just stellar views, but also offers contemporary relief from the aged woods of the main building and the tatami-mat guest rooms, blending modern touches with traditional ryokan surrounds—a common design theme found in the thirteen KAI properties across Japan.

Another of the key concepts of the KAI brand is the incorporation of local traditions and flavors, and in Atami's case that most notably means tapping into local seafood. The multi-course *kaiseki* dinner, served in-room, eaten cross-legged at a low table on tatami, varies by season but is always heavy on freshly caught fish and shellfish, with signature dishes like whole red snapper and clams steamed in eight spices that the chefs prepare alongside more traditional *kaiseki* flavors. It also means giving guests the opportunity to experience Atami's renowned geisha traditions at a nightly after-dinner show

Chrysanthemums, or *kiku*, to use the Japanese word, are a noble flower in Japan. Not only is one used on the Imperial Family's seal, the flower is also said to represent longevity and rejuvenation. In that respect, it's a fitting choice to have them floating on the KAI Atami's natural hot-spring baths, which themselves (according to Japanese tradition) can alleviate numerous ailments and rejuvenate both physically and mentally.

where geisha perform traditional dances and songs, before playing imperial court games with guests, such as the surprisingly addictive fan-throwing. It might sound touristy, but bear in mind that geisha go through years of training to perfect their arts, their movements, and each and every manner; and despite geisha playing a prominent role in guidebook and travel brochure imagery, to actually spend time being entertained by one is an experience usually out of reach of travelers to Japan (and most Japanese). Like staying in a historic ryokan, it's an opportunity to absorb and interact with tradition, not just observe it from afar.

As with all the best ryokan, it would be tempting not to leave the KAI Atami during a stay, but Atami does have some attractions that are worth exploring. The two market streets leading away from Atami Station are something of a must-see for foodies, home to stalls specializing in all sorts of dried fish (all specialties of Shizuoka Prefecture) as well as Japanese sweets, and local fruits and vegetables. Then there is the MOA Museum with its 3,500 or so paintings, its Noh theater, and its gilded tearoom, all set atop the hill that overlooks Atami Station and provides sweeping views over Sagami Bay—a sight almost as impressive as watching the sunset while soaking in one of the KAI's outdoor baths.

KAI Atami 界 熱海
Address: 759 Izusan, Atami, Shizuoka, Japan 413-0002
Telephone: 0570-073-011
Website: : www.hoshinoresorts.com/en/resortsandhotels/kai/atami-ryokan
Email: info@Kai-atami.jp
Number of rooms: 16
Room rate: ¥¥¥

A staff member serving the signature red snapper dish. Staff at the KAI Atami and other Hoshino Resorts properties don't wear traditional clothing like kimono, but rather a uniform that feels like a blend of contemporary and tradition, much like the Hoshino ryokan themselves.

Left No, it's not the same bath again. Both the large wooden communal tubs at the KAI look similar and are decorated with flowers. The difference is that they are gender-separated baths— men and women here bathe apart (as is typical at any ryokan) but both get great views and a similarly luxurious bathing experience.

Below Seasonal is key with *kaiseki*. In autumn, the KAI Atami will serve *matsutake* mushroom in a variety of ways, including in a soup that brings out the *matsutake*'s full earthiness.

Far left The guest rooms represent simple, minimalist Japanese tradition at its very best.

Left The outdoor lounge area, located halfway between the two outdoor baths, has great views and a fridge stocked with complimentary beer and other drinks— ideal post bath.

Left You often hear of ryokan being in tune with nature, but this takes that a step beyond. This tree has been in-situ for hundreds of years and the ryokan has grown around it. It actually grows through a hallway in the lower part of the complex.

Fall colors surround the Yagyu-no-Sho. Year round, this exclusive ryokan is immersed in beautiful surrounds, and on the inside—from the air of calm through to the traditional designs and finely honed hospitality—it's a classic ryokan.

There's something deeply restful and calming about a ryokan like the Yagyu-no-Sho. When you pass through the curtained entrance into quiet, understated surroundings, you feel as though you've stepped into a different Japan—a million miles from the hectic

The Matsu-no-O villa suite has its own little garden, an outdoor bath, and this comfortable spot on the edge of the main tatami room for soaking in the greenery.

modern life of Tokyo and the city's concrete sprawl and back to a world full of subtle refinement, where the best things take their time.

Built in 1970 as a modern take on a teahouse-inspired ryokan, the Yagyu-no-Sho underwent an extensive renovation in 2009 under the guidance of its second-generation owners—Sakiko Hasegawa and her husband Takashi—to make itself more traditional, employing the help of local carpenters, plasterers, and other

craftspeople to bring more natural lighting and lower ceilings to create a more intimate and comfortable space, and add elements like earthen *tataki* flooring in common areas. Walk around the ryokan and you will also find quiet corners with glimpses of landscaped gardens and artistically arranged ikebana accenting hallways (one of the staff is an expert flower arranger).

Tradition extends into the suites, too, all fifteen of which share traits such as tatami flooring and futon instead of beds,

The main entrance to the Yagyu-no-Sho is discreetly hidden among trees, and once inside, the connection to nature doesn't end. The baths, whether communal or private, are surrounded by greenery. With low artificial lighting, natural light comes to the fore in many parts of the building.

Above Ornamental koi in the small pond beside the entrance to the Yagyu-no-Sho.
Left The outdoor baths at the Yagyu-no-Sho are immersed in nature. Silent and calming but for the occasional sound of the woods, they feel even more tranquil when lowly lit at night.

to give just a couple of examples, but are all individually designed. The baths, a key element in a ryokan, vary from room to room, and include outdoor baths, semi-outdoor baths, and indoor baths; all of which are handcrafted by local stone and plaster craftsmen. There are also two villas, with access to their own private gardens.

Away from the rooms, there are also two rocky outdoor communal baths, Musashi-no-Yu and Tsuu-no-Yu, which draw their water from the source under the nearby Shuzenji Temple (see pages 42 and 44 for more about the temple and the Shuzenji area's other sights). As is common with many ryokan, these baths are alternately assigned to male and female guests at different times of the day so guests can try both baths during their stay, soaking away any aches, pains, and stress while immersed in the peace and quiet of nature.

The food is special here, too. With its location in the heart of the Izu Peninsula, Yagyu-no-Sho's head chef Takahashi Shibayama has access to fresh seafood, river fish, and highly prized local produce such as Izu beef, which he turns into a Kyoto-inspired menu of *kaiseki* that changes each month to best utilize seasonal offerings. The dinner could include a seasonal sashimi selection, steak seared on an *onjakuyaki* heated stone grill, grilled sweetfish from the local river served in freshly cut bamboo from the garden, or a *yuzu* citrus stuffed with fish roe, among many other possibilities. Breakfast, which, like dinner, is served in the guests' room, is a classic mix of grilled fish, miso soup, rice, pickles, and a variety of other small dishes made with locally sourced ingredients. And after that, there's plenty of time for another soak in the outdoor bath before checking out.

Yagyu-no-Sho 柳生の庄
Address: 1116-6 Shuzenji, Izu, Shizuoka 410-2416
Telephone: 0558-72-4126
Website: www.yagyu-no-sho.com
Email: info@yagyu-no-sho.com
Number of rooms: 15
Room rate: ¥¥¥¥

Left Not a communal bath, this is one of the private hot-spring baths in the suites, all of which have their own baths, be that indoors, semi open-air, or fully open-air.
Right The natural simplicity of the design even stretches to common areas that in many hotels get little thought.

Above and right Grilled river fish (above) with some subtle aroma and taste added by the use of a small *sudachi* citrus is one of many culinary possibilities with the Yagyu-no-Sho's multi-course dinner. The Izu Peninsula is famed for its seafood, but the vegetables here are excellent, too, as are local beef brands.

SEIRYUSO SHIMODA

A luxury retreat at the southern tip of Izu, the Seiryuso offers some
serious pampering, with spas, fine food, a range of baths, and
moments like this—an in-room private bath with views into nature.

Left The entrance to Seiryuso features one of the largest solid stone lanterns in Japan.
Below The hot-spring baths at the Seiryuso are a mix of private and communal. Most rooms have their own outdoor baths, but there are also options like this public bath.

At ryokan, there is an unspoken rule of etiquette when in the communal hot-spring baths—don't disturb the water too much. At the Seiryuso, things are a little different. They have a hot-spring swimming pool for guests to glide and splash about in. The eighty-foot (twenty-five-meter) pool, surrounded by tropical palms, gives the Seiryuso a grand old look; it seems not so much a ryokan as some old colonial summer retreat one reads about in Agatha Christie novels. Head inside, however, and this ryokan is as traditional and refined as any other.

Take the rooms. The best, Room 102, is a massive 1,345 square feet (125 square meters), and includes a large tatami-matted living room that connects to an outdoor hot-spring bath with views into a private landscaped garden that changes its colors with the seasons. While that's the finest example, even the rooms that don't have their own outdoor baths and gardens, at the very least have indoor hot-spring baths and garden views. And, of course, there are several communal outdoor hot-spring baths (or *rotemburo*, to use the Japanese term) for guests to enjoy. Yet all that aside, there is no escaping that the Seiryuso is not quite your standard ryokan. As well as the pool, there are mosaic-tiled saunas designed with ancient Roman themes, as well as a classically Finnish log-house sauna. There are footbaths, too. And a spa—the Rilissarsi—which offers

Left A swimming pool is certainly not the norm for a ryokan, nor are palm trees. What makes the Seiryuso's pool even more unusual is that it is full of hot-spring water. And, yes, you can swim in it, without having to fully strip off like you would for a bath.

treatments that run from simple foot massages to anti-aging facials.

With its location at the far south of the Izu Peninsula, the Seiryuso has access to extremely fresh, high-quality seafood, which forms the basis of the *kaiseki* dinners. You're likely to enjoy locally caught delicacies such as red snapper, abalone, and lobster along with other regional, seasonal produce. Located just to the north of the coastal town of Shimoda, you're a in a prime area for exploring some of Izu's best sights, including the picturesque white sands of Shirahama Beach; Shimoda Aquarium; and temples like Gyokusenji, Hofukuji, and Ryosenji.

The latter temple—though far from grand in appearance—has its place indelibly marked in the modern history of Japan, as it was here in 1854, after the naval ships of Commodore Perry forced their way into Shimoda Bay, that Japan and the United States signed a treaty that paved the way for Japan to open itself to the world after centuries of self-imposed isolation. That's why a replica of one of Perry's "black ships" (as the Japanese called them at the time) now does tours of the bay, and why there is an annual Black Ship Festival to celebrate Shimoda's place in history.

Seiryuso 清流荘
Address: 2-2 Kochi, Shimoda, Shizuoka 415-0011
Telephone: 0588-22-1361
Website: www.seiryuso.co.jp
Email: info@seiryuso.co.jp
Number of rooms: 26
Room rate: ¥¥¥

Top Many of the rooms combine flooring and beds with more typical Japanese design elements, although there are fully Japanese-style rooms available for purists.
Above Being at the far end of the Izu Peninsula, Seiryuso's chefs have access to an array of top-quality seafood.

TOKIWA HOTEL KOFU

The Tokiwa is proof that big can still be beautiful. With fifty
traditionally appointed rooms and cottages plus striking landscaping,
this founding member of the Japan Ryokan Association is full of charm.

Built around a classic landscape garden and blessed with natural hot-spring waters that come unadulterated straight from their source, the Tokiwa Hotel in the Yumura area of Yamanashi Prefecture—78 miles (126 kilometers) west of Tokyo—has garnered a reputation over the years as a retreat for members of the Imperial Family, Japanese literati, foreign dignitaries, and numerous other VIPs.

Opened in 1929 as an inaugural member of the Japan Ryokan Association, the Tokiwa was one of the first half dozen ryokan in Japan to be registered as an "international tourist ryokan" with the Ministry of Land, Infrastructure, Transport and Tourism. For decades it has been serving guests in English, yet (thankfully) still offers a fully traditional Japanese experience.

That includes the evening meal, which under executive chef Hideji Ono is a multi-course *kaiseki*, a feast for the eyes as much as for the belly, that features fresh seasonal produce and local specialties such as marbled Koshu beef and pork from pigs fed with wine lees to give a strong umami flavor. It includes the fifty guest rooms, which at the Tokiwa are a mix of private cottages and more conventional ryokan rooms that are mostly traditional in design and come with views of a large Japanese garden courtyard. Beyond the courtyard,

from the east wing, Japan's southern alps can be seen and, from the west wing, the near-perfect symmetry of Mount Fuji. Each room is a treat, but it's the eleven cottage rooms (spread across seven cottages) that really stand out, for the additional privacy they afford.

Like the other rooms, the cottages are designed around classic traditional themes (tatami, low table, paper screen doors, and the like) but each brings its own subtle differences, most notably with regard to the baths. The Yakumo room, for example,

Built at the onset of the *Showa* era in the late 1920s, largely with foreign travelers in mind, it's amazing that the Tokiwa is so undiluted in terms of the authenticity of its design. Unlike many other hotels that appeal to overseas travelers, it's still 100 percent Japanese.

Far left The quality of the gardens at the Tokiwa is a defining feature, one that can be enjoyed from the baths, rooms, and common areas such as the comfy couches in the lobby.
Left The cottages are spacious, and appointed in classic ryokan traditions. Yet, they also have a rustic touch or two—look at the tree trunk pillar by the *tokonoma* alcove.
Below The gardens aren't only for looking at. Guests can enjoy a sunny afternoon tea in part of them, too.

comes with a stone-carved private outdoor bath. This room also enjoys pond-side garden views. The Wakatake and Wakamatsu rooms both have outside *hinoki* cypress bath tubs that give off a distinctly sweet yet gentle aroma. The Misaka room has an outdoor *butai-zukuri* tub, on a stage-like platform, while the Shirane room's bath is set in a small *hakoniwa* (box garden). This room also happens to be where the author Seicho Matsumoto stayed while he wrote the mystery *Tower of Waves*—one of many connections the Tokiwa has to literati.

In fact, stroll through the garden and you'll discover more literary connections. Masuji Ibuse, the author of *Black Rain*, is said to have whiled away many an afternoon under the zelkova trees here, while popular Showa-era (1926–1989) novelist and essayist Hitomi Yamaguchi—a

regular in the Kokonoe cottage—wrote about the Tokiwa and its quince trees.

The nearby Yumura Onsen, from where the Tokiwa draws its bathing waters, has a long history. At one time it is said to have been the "secret bath" of Shingen Takeda, the famed *daimyo* (feudal lord) of the Takeda clan during the latter stages of Japan's Sengoku period (1467–1603). Like other hot springs it boasts of healing and restorative properties for ailments ranging from neuralgia to piles. That's something guests can test out at the gender-separated communal baths, where men can enjoy the views through a panoramic window in a wood-paneled bathhouse or from an outdoor pool, and women have the option of either a fragrant open-air bath made of *hinoki* cypress or an indoor bath looking through large windows that frame a mass of greenery.

Tokiwa Hotel 常盤ホテル
Address: 2-5-21 Yumura, Kofu, Yamanashi 400-0073
Telephone: 055-254-3111
Website: www.tokiwa-hotel.co.jp
Email: Via an online form
Number of rooms: 50
Room rate: ¥¥¥

KAI NIKKO LAKE CHUZENJI, NIKKO

In the woods that enshroud Lake Chuzenji, removed from the crowds that flock to Nikko's World Heritage sites yet close enough to easily visit, the KAI Nikko has a fine natural setting to match the quality of ryokan itself.

Nature, history, and indulgence—the KAI Nikko combines all three. Just a few hours north of Tokyo, the ryokan is in the heart of the Nikko region, a popular overnight or day-trip destination, primarily for its UNESCO World Heritage-designated Toshogu Shrine complex. Lake Chuzenji, on whose shores the ryokan sits, was formed by volcanic activity some twenty thousand years ago after an eruption of the area's most prominent (and now dormant) peak, the 8,156-foot (2,486-meter) Mount Nantai, creating picture postcard scenery that is especially stunning in autumn, when the lakeside and surrounding mountains are transformed by colorful foliage.

The windows of the KAI Nikko frame it all; many have views that look out to the lake; the VIP suite goes a step further with views of Lake Chuzenji and Mount Nantai. Looking inward, the rooms are exactly what one would expect from the KAI brand, with varied and stylish combinations of Western and Japanese design sensibilities: there is traditional tatami flooring, there are Western-style beds in place of futon, and there are in-room baths of Japanese cypress or

Above Not all ryokan serve dinner in the rooms, as some don't want to taint the sleeping area with the aroma of food. The KAI Nikko is the same, but it's well worth the short walk from the rooms to the dining area for the *kaiseki*.

Left The journey to the dining area takes guests through this charming roofed corridor, to the sound of sandals "clacking" on the paving.
Right With its lakeside location, the KAI Nikko offers some stunning lake views from rooms and common areas. The area is attractive year-round, but is at its best when autumnal colors come to the fore.

Left The Noh stage near the semi-private dining rooms doesn't host any performances, but it doesn't matter. The highly stylized design and ikebana mimicking the backdrop is one of those unexpected jaw-dropping sights when you first see it.

marble. A closer look reveals many smaller touches. In collaboration with the Nihon Bed company, KAI Hoshino Resorts have developed their own Fuwakumo Sleep beds that adjust to give "the illusion that you are on a cloud", according to KAI. They have also produced their own *yukata* gowns, which unlike the usual cotton gowns found at ryokan are 100 percent linen, a fabric that warms the body in Nikko's cold winters and cools it in the heat of summer.

Dinner and breakfast are both taken in semi-private dining spaces that are reached on a walk that takes guests past an elegantly designed wooden Noh stage. Both meals take guests on a culinary journey that leans heavily on local produce: breakfast features a Nikko favorite, *yuba* (tofu skin), dinner a classic multi-course *kaiseki* that (depending on the season) might involve beef steamed in a stone box, sweet shrimp marinated in aged sake and served in a lime, or grilled conger eel.

In keeping with the concept at KAI of incorporating local traditions into the ryokan experience, after dinner each night staff perform a Nikko *geta* dance, a kind of tap dance routine using a local version of traditional wooden-soled *geta* sandals—something craftsmen in Nikko have been making in a distinctive way for the past four hundred years, from back when the Nikko area's most famous sight, Toshogu Shrine, was still relatively new.

And what of the shrine? A winding forty-minute bus trip down from the mountain (the KAI runs a free service), Toshogu was built to enshrine Tokugawa Ieyasu, the man who united a warring Japan and became the first shogun of the Edo era (1603–1868). Given his gigantic status in Japanese history, perhaps it's no wonder that Toshogu is so strikingly decadent. Its many highlights include a deep red five-story pagoda, and the Yomei-mon roofed gateway, decorated in black, gold, red, and green and accented with five hundred or so intricate carvings of birds, dancing maidens, dragons, and flowers. Just a short stroll from the KAI you can also visit the Kegon Falls, which plunge more than three hundred feet (about one hundred meters) into a lush gorge. But more than anything, there's the KAI itself: a timeless Japanese experience.

Hoshino Resorts KAI Nikko 界 日光
Address: 2482-1 Chugushi, Nikko, Tochigi 321-1661
Telephone: 050-3786-1144
Website: www.hoshinoresorts.com/en/resortsandhotels/kai/nikko
Email: nikko@kai-ryokan.jp
Number of rooms: 33
Room rate: ¥¥¥

Rooms are a blend of Japanese and Western; mostly traditional ryokan in style, with tatami, sliding doors, and other features, but perfectly merged with elements such as polished flooring and beds. Not many ryokan that try to combine the two get it right—the Western part is typically very dated and drab—but the KAI Nikko nails it.

Above left The lounge area by the baths is another special feature. It's vast, with ample space to unwind (pre or post bath) on one of the custom-made cushions on the tatami without really noticing anyone else doing the same.

Above One of the nice small touches at the baths are the cedar balls floating on the water. They give off a gentle, sweet scent as they bob about.

Above An example of the thoughtful accents you find throughout the property, rooms have fresh ikebana arrangements. Absolutely timeless, the finest of ikebana can fit the most traditional setting and the sleek contemporary ones.

Left One of many highlights of the nightly *kaiseki* is the locally sourced beef. Depending on the exact menu, it's sometimes steamed in front of you in a stone box, coming out so succulent that it pretty much melts in the mouth.

In a hot-spring area that feels about as remote as possible so close to Tokyo, the Honke Bankyu is steeped in history, having been in operation since the Heike clan (depicted here in an annual historic reenactment) oversaw this part of Japan in the pre-Edo era.

River. The four-story second building—where the hotel recommends families with small children stay to protect the peace and quiet of the main building—is very similar in design, but with a more modern outward appearance and a slightly brighter feel inside.

Dinner continues the rustic theme. While breakfast is a buffet, the evening meal is served in a large hall dotted with *irori* hearths, around which guests sit on the floor to enjoy local dishes such as char-grilled river fish and hot pots, all of which can be accompanied by a range of regional sake (including cloudy *nigori-shu*) and homemade wines. And just to remind you that you are deep in old Japan, to reach the dining hall, you have to go out of the main building and cross the river over a wobbly vine-weaved bridge that in summer sometimes offers up glimpses of fireflies.

There are baths too, of course, in the shape of a rocky communal outdoor bath set alongside the river, as well as a private bath available for booking, both of which draw on the area's natural hot-spring source and allow guests to immerse themselves not just in water said to soothe ailments like neuralgia, but also in the sights and sounds of the lush riverside.

And while the Bankyu is in a fairly remote location, the area has its share of attractions. In February, when the Bankyu will be carpeted white with snow, there is the local Kamakura Festival, when small igloos will be built, and ice sculptures will be on display at the Bankyu. In summer, you can try catching fish by hand in the river or go firefly spotting. Anyone lucky

Although located in Tochigi, which is only a couple of hours north of Tokyo and home to the UNESCO World Heritage-designated Toshogu Shrine complex, a popular tourist attraction—the Yunishigawa Onsen feels far removed from the pace of modern-day life.

It was here, in the latter part of the twelfth century that the Heike clan retreated and settled after years of war against the Genji clan, and where the two clans finally agreed on peace. It was also here that Heike clan descendants discovered hot-spring waters in the late 1500s and established an inn where travelers could soak in these mineral-rich waters to cure themselves of their ills. Twenty-five generations on, the sons and daughters of the Heike are still running the Honke Bankyu.

Spread across two buildings, the forty-five rooms are traditional yet rustic in style. The main building has plastered walls that are accented by darkly aged beams, tatami flooring, and in some of the higher-end rooms open hearths (called *irori*). Three rooms even come with their own private *rotemburo* (outdoor hot-spring baths) overlooking the babbling Yunishi

enough to come in June gets to experience the Yunishi River's main annual event, the Heike Grand Festival, which sees parades in historical costumes, traditional craft making demonstrations, and even small reenactments of battles between the Heike and the Genji. A visit to the Bankyu is like stepping back in time, whatever the season.

Honke Bankyu 本家伴久
Address: 749 Yunishigawa Onsen, Nikko, Tochigi 321-2601
Telephone: 0288-98-0011
Website: www.bankyu.co.jp/english
Email: info@bankyu.co.jp
Number of rooms: 45
Room rate: ¥¥¥

Above On the way to dinner, guests cross this vine bridge. It's even more interesting after a bit of dinnertime sake.

Above right People have been bathing in these hot springs for more than five hundred years, as long as the Honke Bankyu has been in existence. And for all that time, the ryokan has been in the hands of the same family.

Right and opposite page Book a room in the older main building, if you can. With their heavy, aged beams and simple plastered walls, they have a lovely earthy feel.

Right A ryokan dinner doesn't get any more rustic than sitting around a hearth watching your meal cook on skewers like this.

Once home to a member of the Imperial Family, the Yoshida Sanso retains the intimacy of a private home, but combined with all the refined elements that make a classic ryokan.

Above and opposite page, top Meals come with a gift from the *okami* ("house mother") in the form of *waka*, a classical form of poetry, which she writes out on *washi* paper in a now rare style of calligraphy called *hentaigana*.
Left Light summer screens catch the breeze from the Yoshida Sanso's pretty strolling garden.

Imperial heritage and Kyoto traditions. The Yoshida Sanso is steeped in both. Situated in the foothills of Mount Yoshida, one of the thirty-six often small, but scenic peaks of Kyoto's eastern mountain ranges, the building was constructed in 1932 as the second home of the current Emperor's uncle, who at the time was studying at Kyoto University. It became a ryokan in 1948.

Now designated by the Japanese government as an Important Cultural Asset, the two-story Yoshida Sanso was created by master carpenter Tsunekazu Nishioka, who during his lifetime was given the awards National Cultural

Treasure and Person of Cultural Merit for his restoration work on historic Shinto shrines and Buddhist temples. Nishioka's design for the Yoshida Sanso is certainly quite different from a typical, traditional ryokan, blending architectural touches from both East and West. There is *hinoki* cypress wood used throughout to give a traditional feel, but there are also features like parquetry and art deco-inspired stained glass windows. As a reminder of the building's Imperial roots, you'll also see Imperial chrysanthemum motifs on roof tiles and sliding-door handles, while one

curious design feature comes in the form of a Western-style toilet with tatami-mat flooring—possibly the most unusual example of East meets West ever seen.

Each of the eight- to ten-mat rooms also comes with a view. Upstairs, that means sights such as Mount Hiei and the large Daimonji character on the Nyoigatake peak, which is set alight (and visible from much of the city) as part of the annual Daimonji Gozan Okuribi festival in August. Downstairs rooms open out on to the Yoshida Sanso's lush garden, home to the delicate pinks and whites of cherry blossoms in spring, vibrant azaleas in early summer, and peace and quiet year round, except for the special occasions when special events such as *koto* concerts take place on the lawn.

With just five guest rooms, staying at the Yoshida Sanso is an intimate affair, which is perhaps one reason guests often book for two or three nights, rather than the typical single-night ryokan stay. Another reason is the flexibility of meal offerings—guests don't have to take *kaiseki* every night (though they should try Yoshida Sanso's seasonally inspired multi-course dinner at least once). Whatever the meal, however, one unique touch sees the Yoshida Sanso's *okami* ("house mother") presenting guests with traditional *waka* poetry at dinner, handwritten in beautifully ornate

The entrance. From your first moment at the Yoshida Sanso, you are treated to the work of the master carpenter, Tsunekazu Nishioka, who created this villa for the Imperial Family.

hentaigana, an old yet fading form of calligraphy born in the Heian era some 1,200 years ago.

The area around the ryokan is also full of history with its narrow lanes and small temples and shrines; the kind of area that oozes old-Kyoto charm. About half a mile

Right The first-floor guest rooms have splendid garden views.

Below There are some lovely touches at the Yoshida Sanso. Instead of the more common paper screen doors of other ryokan, the woven-reed effect gives this room a very distinctive look. And for something very unique, search for the toilet on the first floor—it is a standard Western toilet, but on a tatami-mat floor!

to the east is one of Kyoto's most historic temples, the fifteenth-century Ginkakuji, aka the Silver Pavilion (a misleading name given that there isn't an ounce of decoration on it; although its understated natural look is perfect as is). Nearby, the pretty Philosopher's Pathway leads southward to temples such as Honenin and its picturesque mossy gardens, and then on toward major tourist attractions Nanzenji and Heian Jingu, the latter of which is entered under a large vermilion *torii* gateway that can be seen in the distance from the Yoshida Sanso's second floor. As we said: steeped in history.

Yoshida Sanso 吉田山荘

Address: 59 1 Yoshida Shimo-ooji-cho, Sakyo-ku, Kyoto 606-8314
Telephone: 075-771-6125
Website: www.yoshidasanso.com
Email: ask@yoshidasanso.com
Number of rooms: 5
Room rate: ¥¥¥¥

Below left Tradition moves through generation after generation in Kyoto. The Yoshida Sanso's *okami* ("house mother") and her daughter, the future *okami*.

Below *Geta* sandals for exploring the garden. They take a little getting used to walking in as you go from slab to slab, but that makes you take your time and allows you to enjoy the garden even more.

One of the screens at the Aoi Kamogawa-Tei offers a glimpse
of old Kyoto, much like a night in this old *machiya* townhouse.

A traditional Kyoto *machiya* townhouse for the twenty-first century, the hundred-year-old Aoi Kamogawa-Tei is an intriguing blend of old and new with an equally intriguing history—it's a former sake storage house that later became the home of *maiko* apprentice geisha working in Kyoto's old Pontocho geisha district.

Although at heart this old town house is still distinctly Japanese, it is obviously now very different from its *maiko* days. Step inside the first-floor living room, for example, and you are met with a raised tatami-mat section with a low rectangular table at its center, next to which comes modern wooden flooring, a leather couch and a white wall accented by a long and richly decorated traditional screen painting. Upstairs, there are two Japanese-style bedrooms; one that has futon for sleeping and the other which has beds—a nod to the mix of design elements from East and West. Next to the bedrooms is a riverside library, where guests can pick up a book and relax on a lounger with views out over the Kamogawa, the main river running through Kyoto.

As the Aoi Kamogawa-Tei is a *machiya* rather than a ryokan, there is no provision of elaborate *kaiseki* dinners, which helps to keep your stay reasonably priced and also means you can go out and explore Kyoto's culinary scene. With the Aoi Kamogawa-Tei's central location you are only minutes away from dozens of great places to eat for a variety of budgets. For guests who prefer to eat at the *machiya*—breakfast, lunch, or dinner can be ordered in for guests from the many restaurants in the area. Otherwise, you can stroll north to places like Nishiki-koji—Kyoto's oldest food market—or head for one of the department store food basements along Shijo-dori to pick up a bento lunch box or something else ready-made to take back to the *machiya*. Both are within easy walking distance.

Looking at the rest of the immediate area, the Aoi Kamogawa-Tei can certainly claim to have a good location for taking in many of central Kyoto's main sights. First,

Left Located next to Kyoto's main river, the Kamogawa, from which it takes part of its name, the Aoi doesn't just have pleasant views, it has a tremendous central location within easy walking distance of areas like the historic Nishiki-koji market, the restaurants of Pontocho, and the Gion geisha district.

Right Not geisha (or *geiko* to use the Kyoto term) or *maiko* (trainee geisha), but in this part of central Kyoto it isn't at all unusual to see people dressed up in fine kimono, whether that's for work at a ryokan or restaurant, for a special occasion, or just for the sheer enjoyment of it—and why not in such a lovely traditional setting?

the *machiya* is set directly alongside the Kamogawa River, a popular area for a stroll or just chilling out for an hour or two. From there, guests can cross the river and then head fifteen minutes or so northeast to the Gion geisha district, a lovely area defined by old wooden buildings that now house everything from exclusive restaurants to casual eateries. As well as visiting Nishiki-koji market, you can also take in the traditional stores in the covered Teramachi arcade, which runs north from Nishiki-koji's eastern end. And being within ten minutes of several stations, not to mention main bus routes, you are also in easy striking distance of most of Kyoto's top attractions, although you could easily be forgiven for just hanging out in the peace and quiet of the *machiya* all day.

Aoi Kamogawa-Tei 葵 鴨川邸
Address (central office): 145-1 Tennocho, Shimogyo-ku, Kyoto 600-8013
Telephone: 075-354-7770
Website: en.kyoto-stay.jp
Email: aoi@kyoto-stay.jp
Number of rooms: One rental house that can accommodate up to five people.
Room rate: ¥¥¥¥ (per house, no meals)

Above right A pair of Buddhist traditional guardian *shishi* lion statues protect the main entrance.
Right In keeping with Japanese aesthetics, the subtle details at the Aoi have a major impact on the overall ambience.
Below right There's an intriguing merging of tradition with touches of contemporary at all of the Aoi's *machiya* properties—the furnishing here is modern, but blends both new and old sensibilities.

GION HATANAKA CENTRAL KYOTO

The Hatanaka looks very much like a typical high-end Kyoto ryokan, but beyond the pretty garden and charming interiors is a ryokan that offers an unusually deep Kyoto experience in other regards, with nightly *maiko* shows over fine dining.

Blending into the charming side streets that define the area between the Yasaka Shrine and the Gion geisha district, the Hatanaka is in a prime location for exploring some of central Kyoto's most historic sights.

Classic ryokan with a theatrical twist. If you had to sum up the Gion Hatanaka in a single sentence, that would be it. To look at, the Gion Hatanaka certainly has all the ryokan boxes ticked, with spacious and bright tatami-mat guest rooms featuring views onto bamboo gardens that are framed by paper screen doors, not to mention the calligraphic scroll hanging in the *tokonoma* alcove and the low rectangular table catching reflections in its polished finish. The tradition continues with large communal baths, while each room has an en-suite aromatic cypress bathtub.

The culinary offerings here also fall into the classic category. As you might well expect from a Kyoto ryokan, dinner at the Gion Hatanaka is a reflection of the city's long-established *kaiseki* traditions, with a succession of small dishes that utilize local, seasonal produce and also draw heavily on Kyoto's vegetarian Buddhist influences. In spring you might be served bamboo shoots from Kyoto's Nishiyama region; in summer highly sought-after *hamo* (pike). In autumn, when many would argue Japanese cuisine rises to its greatest heights, there will be earthy *matsutake* mushrooms, perhaps grilled, maybe in a soup, and then winter will see delicacies such as snow crab worked into the menu. Even the most basic of store-cupboard ingredients are sourced with care here: soy sauce comes from Sawai in Kyoto and from Shodoshima in Shikoku; sea salt comes from the Nanki region; Kinuhikari rice comes from Tanba; Mikawa mirin comes from Aichi—a veritable who's who of Japanese produce.

While the style and presentation of the food is classic Kyoto, what makes the Gion Hatanaka quite different to most other Kyoto ryokan is the focus on entertainment. This ryokan is famous for its optional "dining with *maiko*" evenings, where apprentice geisha (called *maiko*) perform traditional dances, play the koto, serve sake, and chat to guests as they eat dinner—a rare opportunity to peek inside the otherwise hard-to-penetrate world of the geisha. On top of that, the Gion Hatanaka even has nights where the *kaiseki* comes accompanied with *kembu* sword dances and opportunities to learn about the life of the samurai (and get your hands on their swords).

The Gion Hatanaka is located approximately ten minutes from Gion-Shijo Station and Hankyu Kawaramachi Station, a prime position to take in the attractions of central Kyoto and the Higashiyama area. Immediately to the north, there is Yasaka Shrine, founded in the 650s and the current-day host of the Gion Matsuri every July. This is Kyoto's largest festival, which at its peak sees processions of floats and portable shrines winding around the city streets. The pretty Gion area, with its teahouses and geisha, is only a short walk to the west, as are the shops in and around Shijo-dori and Kawaramachi. Continue walking in that direction and you will come to the covered Nishiki-koji food market, which teems with small stores specializing in all sorts of local produce and even cooking utensils. Alternatively, head south, via some of Kyoto's most charming old alleyways and

sloping streets, and you'll find the UNESCO World Heritage–designated Kiyomizu Temple. The whole is experience is deep, deep Kyoto.

Gion Hatanaka 祇園畑中

Address: 505 Gion Minamigawa, Higashiyama-ku, Kyoto 605-0074

Telephone: 075-541-5315

Website: www.thehatanaka.co.jp

Email: kyoto@thehatanaka.co.jp

Number of rooms: 23

Room rate: ¥¥¥¥

Above The dinner shows at the Hatanaka, which are open to non-guests, are a highlight of a stay—a rare opportunity to enjoy an up-close performance by local *maiko* of traditional music and dance.
Right The rooms might not be the biggest, but aesthetically they are the epitome of a classic ryokan.
Below The *kaiseki* dinner is, of course, seasonal, but so is the presentation, with decorative touches like this leaf as a lid on a dish shaped from bamboo.

The Hiiragiya is one of the oldest and best-known ryokan in Kyoto, built in 1818 and run by the same family ever since. The ryokan has two wings—an old and a new one (whose central courtyard garden is shown here).

Above The stone paved entrance to the Hiiragiya, accented by ikebana arrangments, transports you back in time.

Below One of the oldest rooms at the Hiiragiya and one of the most enchanting, with its gently aged interiors and mossy private garden. It's not hard to understand why 1968 Nobel Prize for Literature winner, Yasunari Kawabata, would request this room on his numerous stays here.

The 1968 Nobel Prize laureate for literature, Yasunari Kawabata, once wrote of the Hiiragiya, "It is here … that I wistfully recall that sense of tranquility that belonged to old Japan". Were Kawabata still with us and still calling the Hiiragiya in Kyoto his regular home away from home, I can't imagine his feelings would have changed at all. Old Japan has been preserved here in ways few other ryokan could emulate.

The Hiiragiya was built in 1818 and has always been run by the same family. Like many of Kyoto's ryokan, its life began not as an inn for paying guests, but as a place where merchants would be hosted by the family they were trading with. As the Hiiragiya's sixth-generation *okami* ("house mother"), Akemi Nishimura, explains, the essence of the service one finds today at traditional ryokan stems from that sense of welcoming a guest into the home and treating them as one of the family, giving them the feeling of "returning home" rather than checking in; and with that the *okami*'s role has developed into that of surrogate mother to everyone staying. The Hiiragiya has seen generations of *okami* function as surrogate mothers to an incredible list of dignitaries, literati, and

celebrities, from Oscar winners and laureates to royalty and politicians.

Four of the Hiiragiya's rooms are thought to date back to its original construction, and it is in one of these rooms that Kawabata was inspired by the tranquility and timelessness to sit and write. Today these rooms can be enjoyed for their classic ryokan interiors: tatami-mat flooring, paper screen doors, aging wood tones, and Hiiragiya signature touches such as *ajirou* woven-reed ceilings and decorated *fusuma* door panels from the Edo era (1603–1868), the latter of which are now designated as important cultural properties. Many rooms open out onto or at least have views over small, ornate gardens, accented with dark moss and stepping stones. The Hiiragiya gives easy access to some of Kyoto's most famous attractions—Nijo Castle and Kyoto Imperial Palace Park are just short walks away—but you almost have to force yourself to leave its rooms to go explore.

In the seven rooms in the brighter new wing, which was reconstructed in 2006, the defining features vary, but all have been added to the Hiiragiya with tradition and craftsmanship firmly in mind. One room

Above The rooms in the newer wing have a contemporary feel, but everything from the design and the artisans employed to create them are deeply rooted in tradition.

Left Many older rooms have screen doors that are listed as national cultural assets. This ryokan is noted too for the service standards of its experienced *okami* (landladies), who are said to be almost "surrogate mothers" for the guests.

Right One of the first few dishes that comes with the multi-course *kaiseki*. The exact line-up of dishes changes depending on what's in season, but whatever is on the menu will be sublime.

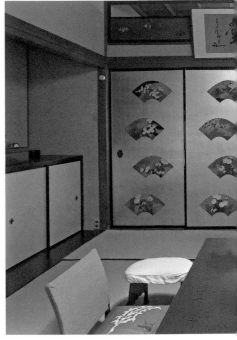

Above The framing of miniature gardens or garden views is a classic touch that's been incorporated into the rooms in the new wing.
Above right As is often the case with the older Kyoto ryokan, some rooms can be small, so be sure to request one of the larger ones if that's important to you, but even in the smallest you'll find many fascinating details. The fans on this Edo-era screen door are made with crushed shells and when you look closely are raised.

has an outdoor moon-viewing deck extending from its main tatami area, others have wooden screens in the *tokonoma* alcove that slide open to reveal glimpses of traditional garden design. As Mrs. Nishimura puts it, "The theme is to merge old with new; using lighter, fresher colors,

but traditional designs and skills." One room displays the work of Living National Treasure, craftsman Kiyotsugu Nakagawa. He has used thousand-year-old *jindai* cedar, which is buried underground until semi-petrified and almost a light grey in color, to do woodworking on the walls and skirting that features perfectly aligned straight grains.

The food at the Hiiragiya is classic *Kyo-ryori* (Kyoto-style cuisine), whose twelve courses are served in-room, delivered like works of art on fine ceramics and lacquerware, starting with an aperitif of local sake and then over a couple of hours winding its way through a platter of seasonal appetizers (like simmered

eggplant and beef sirloin in a delicate *dashi* soup with ginger) and on to such delicacies as conger eel with turnip, burdock, and chrysanthemum accented with a *yuzu* miso. Timeless cuisine for a timeless experience.

Hiiragiya 柊家
Address: Nakahakusancho, Fuyacho Anekoji-agaru, Nakagyo-ku, Kyoto 604-8094
Telephone: 075-221-1136
Website: www.hiiragiya.co.jp
Email: info@hiiragiya.co.jp
Number of rooms: 28
Room rate: ¥¥¥¥

Right and below Many of the rooms in the original building either open on to their own small gardens or have garden views. Like a starry night sky, the longer you look at the gardens, the more details come to light—most obviously the stone stupas and aged mossy patches, but also elements like the little stones placed discreetly on some pathways to indicate one shouldn't go beyond that point.

Above The best baths are in the new wing, which have aromatic wood tubs perfect for a long soak after exploring Kyoto.

KINMATA CENTRAL KYOTO

An oasis of tradition in another modern side street in central Kyoto. Go beyond the stupa at the entrance and the transformation from new to old is sudden and stunning.

Founded in 1801 and now located in a *machiya* townhouse in the heart of Kyoto, the Kinmata is pure Kyoto, a cocoon in which to shelter from the modern world—a place to immerse oneself deep in tradition, to soak up Japanese aesthetics and hospitality, and to sample the best of the former capital's culinary heritage.

The building itself, which is now designated as a National Tangible Cultural Property by the Japanese government, is pure vintage Kyoto. The seven guest rooms open onto or overlook a small landscaped garden, which, when observed from your seat at the low, lacquered table in the center of the tatami-matted room, is framed by sliding paper screen doors. Except in Kyoto's siesta-inducing summers, that is, when the doors are replaced with traditional reed screens to allow natural

Left Step up into the lobby and you are greeted with a gentle creak; the building's way of reminding you of its age. Throughout, the ryokan is growing old gracefully, one of Kyoto's grand old dames.
Right The landscaped garden is small, but beautiful, and visible from all the rooms.

Left The façade of the Kinmata has to be one of the prettiest in Japan. It's the kind of *machiya* townhouse that screams "old Kyoto". So, it's not surprising that the building is now designated as a Tangible Cultural Property.

ventilation and cooling—a classic example of how old Japanese buildings were designed to adapt to the changing seasons long before the advent of electricity.

The owner here is a chef, and its cuisine is a specialty—that's why the Kinmata refers to itself as a *ryori-ryokan* (literally, a "food ryokan"). In fact, the Kinmata also functions as a highly rated *kaiseki* restaurant, opening its dining room to non-guests for both lunch and dinner. For guests, the seasonally changing, multi-course meals are served in-room or in the main dining room, depending on the guests' preference, using an antique collection of fine ceramics and lacquerware that has been handed down and added to

through half a dozen generations. In spring, you can expect dishes to include something like baked red snapper, perhaps in a dish with a seasonally matching cherry-blossom motif, while in summer you might be treated to sea eel served as sushi or in a palette-refreshing clear soup. Autumn then brings highly prized *matsutake* mushrooms, which could be grilled with shrimp or served in a rich broth, and then in winter one might be treated to mackerel grilled between planks of cedar. And if that piques an interest in Japanese cooking, guests can also sign up for a *kaiseki* cooking lesson with the Kinmata's chefs.

The location is also in something of a foodie hotspot. The Kinmata is just off the eastern end of the covered Nishiki-koji market, the oldest food market in Kyoto, dating back to the 1600s. The market is located in a single, narrow street that is

home to more than a hundred shops specializing in everything from dried and cured seafood, pickles, tofu, traditional sweets, seasonal vegetables, and even cooking utensils. Running northward from there, the Teramachi arcade is another old shopping street, where stores selling everyday provisions stand alongside places selling traditional goods such as incense, Buddhist statues and paraphernalia, and antiques. Then a block to the south is the modern and bustling Shijo-dori, from where buses and trains run to almost all parts of the city, and from where it's easy to get your bearings and set off on foot to explore several of Kyoto's most popular attractions—be that a stroll around the nearby Gion entertainment district (known for its geisha and old teahouses), a kabuki performance at the historic Minami-za Theater, or a look at ancient religious sites such as Yasaka Shrine or Chion-in Temple.

Above and below The classic interiors of the guest rooms, with the garden framed by sliding doors, are the ideal setting for an elaborate *kaiseki* dinner taken at a low table on tatami.

Kinmata 近又
Address: 407 Gokomachi, Shijo-agaru, Nakagyo-ku, Kyoto 604-8044
Telephone: 075-221-1039
Website: www.kinmata.com
Email: kaiseki@kinmata.com
Number of rooms: 7
Room rate: ¥¥¥

There's no mistaking the brewery heritage. From the decorative sake barrels to the old brewing equipment that still decorates much of this lovely private rental, the Kinpyo is immersed in its past.

You can even spot the sake-brewing roots from the outside. When this was still a brewery, the *sugidama* cedar ball now hanging from the eaves would have been hung outside to announce that a new batch of sake was ready for sale. Starting off green, the *sugidama* would then gradually turn brown, its own aging process showing the age and freshness of the sake available.

Opposite page, above The view from the small library upstairs. The high-vaulted ceiling and rough walls (employing earthenware), not to mention the richly aging woods, are just a few of the original design elements that make the Kinpyo so atmospheric.

Historic. Refined. Rustic. Contemporary. Elegant. The ryokan comes in many guises. It isn't, however, the only form of traditional accommodation in Japan. At a more casual, typically smaller, and affordable level, you have family-run *minshuku*—somewhat akin to a bed-and-breakfast—while temple-run accommodation (called *shukubo*) can also come close to a ryokan experience, which isn't surprising given that many ryokan began life as temple lodgings. Then you have another variation, old townhouses called *machiya*, which can

be rented. And the Kinpyo is one of the most charming *machiya* of them all.

Occupying a two-story, nineteenth-century building that once functioned as a sake brewery, the Kinpyo greets visitors with dark, aged timbers and high-vaulted ceilings that are punctuated by small square windows pierced by shards of light. Closer inspection reveals distinctive rough earthen walls and antique furnishings—apt, considering the Kinpyo is only steps away from several dozen antique stores on Furumonzen and Shinmonzen Streets that make this part of Kyoto one of the best places in Japan to go hunting for antique ceramics, lacquerware, furniture, tea utensils, and many other traditional objects. Given the sake heritage, it should also come as no surprise that sake paraphernalia is scattered around the property too; there are ceramic sake servers, straw-wrapped sake barrels, and several awards certifying the quality of the sake produced by the family that owns the Kinpyo. All combined, first impressions are that you are going to be living—albeit briefly—deep in Kyoto's past.

The Kinpyo keeps with ryokan tradition with an aromatic *hinoki* cypress bathtub that overlooks a classic *machiya* feature, a tiny courtyard garden. Next to it, the bedroom features plump futon on a tatami-mat floor, and next door to that comes a small tatami-mat lounge area with a low table, richly ornate screen painting, and a sloping ceiling that invites a head bump or two—all classic *machiya*.

The main difference between staying in a *machiya* and staying in a ryokan, apart

Left The second floor living room—along with a quaint sloping ceiling—is defined by this vivid screen painting, which provides a rather regal backdrop when relaxing at the low table with a little sake or some green tea.

from the privacy of having a house all to yourself, is the food. The Kinpyo, in common with other *machiya*, doesn't serve meals, and that opens the door to all sorts of possibilities. First, it can make the stay more affordable than many ryokan, as you are paying for lodgings only. Beyond that, it allows for variety—if you are staying more than a night, *kaiseki* dinners (as wonderful as they are) can begin to get too much. At the Kinpyo, the English-speaking owners can arrange for several of the traditional restaurants in the neighborhood to deliver dinner, but even better is to head out and explore Kyoto's dining scene. A ten-minute walk away you'll find many reasonably priced restaurants along Shijo-dori. Or you could delve into more traditional options on the charming Pontocho Alley. The Kinpyo is also just to the north of Kyoto's Gion district, known for its old teahouses and geisha, and—just like the Kinpyo—its old-Kyoto feel.

Gion–Kinpyo 金瓢

Address: 335 Miyoshi-cho, Furumonzen, Higashiyama-ku, Kyoto 605-0081

Telephone: 075-708-5143

Website: http://www.kinpyo.jp

Email: info@kinpyo.jp

Number of rooms: Single rental house for two to six people

Room rate: ¥¥¥¥ (per house, no meals)

Left The Kinpyo is a very historic property that oozes old charm, but with touches like this swanky metal sink (among others) it has been gently modernized in places to make it comfortable, too.

Above As initial views go when one first steps into a rental property, it's hard to beat the impact of the Kinpyo. It's the perfect way to stay in an ancient capital so steeped in history as Kyoto.

Above Next to the entrance, this multi-purpose downstairs room celebrates the Kinpyo's sake roots. There are old advertising signs on the wall for the brews once made here, along with awards and bottles of the brewery's current offerings, which are now made elsewhere.

Left The Gion district—a good place for a spot of geisha spotting—is just a short walk away from the Kinpyo, as are some of the best dining areas and antique stores, among other attractions.

Like the finest of small ryokan, entering the Seikoro Inn feels like setting foot inside someone's home. And that goes to the heart of ryokan hospitality—being cared for (albeit formally) like a member of the family.

If you were to select a hotel just by the appearance of its website, the clashing colors and homemade look of the Seikoro Inn's online presence would very likely have you booking elsewhere, but this is one ryokan that definitely shouldn't be judged by its digital cover. The Seikoro Inn is one of the finest examples of a Meiji-era (1868–1912) ryokan in Kyoto.

The Seikoro Inn began life in a different building in 1831 as a *hatago*, a simple form of lodging for merchants and travelers that was a forerunner to the ryokan. In 1901, the current Seikoro was created as a sub-branch to the original building, and ever since then it has been run by the Shiroyama family.

Recently, an annex of nine traditional-style rooms has been added to the existing thirteen rooms, but it's the original rooms that allow one to immerse oneself fully in old Kyoto. The old rooms on the second-floor look out over the Seikoro Inn's leafy garden, which is accented with stone stupas and sculptures, while the old rooms on the first floor open onto it, allowing you to step out into private pockets of nature. The interior design of the inn, like the garden, is largely traditional, with sliding paper screen doors, richly hand-painted screens, and tatami matting, along with features like near-reflective lacquerware tables inlaid with mother-of-pearl and subtle ikebana flower arrangements. But with that also come European antique furniture and ornaments in some of the common areas, giving the Seikoro Inn an almost Victorian feel in places.

Each room has its own small bath and there are two communal tubs made with gently aromatic four-hundred-year-old *koyamaki* (umbrella pine), although as is normal in central Kyoto the water for these doesn't come from a hot-spring source.

Unlike many ryokan, dinner is not compulsory here, making the Seikoro Inn one of the more affordable of Kyoto's high-end properties. Guests can opt for an accommodation plan that includes a multi-course *kaiseki* meal, or they can choose half-board, or board only. It's an uncommon, but welcome flexibility that makes the inn attractive to guests staying more than one night or who want to go out and explore Kyoto's culinary scene.

Location-wise, the Seikoro Inn enjoys the calm of a quiet side street near the Kamogawa River in the southern part of Kyoto's Higashiyama area, a twenty-minute walk west of the World Heritage-designated Kiyomizu Temple and just a few minutes from public transportation that opens up all of Kyoto's old and more recent attractions—places on and off the beaten path that the English-speaking owner is happy to direct guests to.

Seikoro Inn 晴鴨樓
Address: Tonyamachi-dori, Gojo-sagaru, Higashiyama-ku, Kyoto 605-0907
Telephone: 075-561-0771
Website: www.seikoro.com
Email: info@seikoro.com
Number of rooms: 22 in all, 13 dating back to 1901 (one of which has a bed, not futon) and 9 in a newer annex.
Room rate: ¥¥¥

Far left The Meiji era (1868–1912) saw Japan opening itself to the rest of the world and an influx of Western influences, which included European architecture. Outside of the tatami-matted guest rooms, you can see plenty of that at the Seikoro.
Left One of the rooms in the oldest part of the Seikoro Inn, which dates back to 1901.

Above In this room in the new annex, you can see modern Western influences with the couches and wooden flooring. There are also some unusual traditional features—check out the round red lacquer table, instead of the more typical and understated rectangular table.
Right Communal baths tends to be quite modest in size in Kyoto's older city-center ryokan, but nevertheless the craftsmanship of the tubs is frequently very special. This one was handcrafted from aromatic cedar.

A sleek retreat from the stresses of modern living that's set just upriver from the popular Arashiyama area, the Hoshinoya Kyoto fuses the finest of classic ryokan elements with those of an exclusive five-star resort.

The Arashiyama area in western Kyoto was once a retreat for the aristocracy, a place of calm and tranquility surrounded by nature, somewhere to unwind and appreciate the four seasons—the pinks of cherry blossoms in spring, the verdant and luscious summer, the earthy reds and yellows that engulf the area's riverside in fall, and the white-dappled starkness of winter.

Today, Arashiyama is more famous as one of Kyoto's main sightseeing destinations, attracting hordes of tourists to its iconic bamboo grove and its historic sites that include Tenryuji, a World Heritage-designated temple established in the 1300s. But it still has its pockets of calm. It has the Hoshinoya Kyoto.

The ryokan is reached via a sedate ten-minute boat ride up the picturesque Katsuura River, leaving the tourist crowds behind. A luxurious blend of traditional and contemporary, the Hoshinoya Kyoto was opened in 2009 in a renovated hundred-year-old building that was originally the private residence of business tycoon Ryoi Suminokura, but which has been gently modernized in a style that the Hoshinoya describes as "contemporary, but with one foot firmly placed in the past".

That concept is most obvious in guest rooms, which vary in exact layout and appearance, but all share defining design features, with elements such as *karakami* wall prints produced with 130-year-old woodblocks using a mixture of chalk, sanguine, ocher, black ink, mica, and other pigments—a classic craft utilized to lend a contemporary Japanese feel. Likewise, the paper screen doors are given a modern twist with glass rather than paper, and angular crosspieces. While rooms feature a mix of tatami and wooden flooring that oozes tradition, furnishings include sleek beds instead of futon and locally handcrafted floor-level sofas. All rooms have views over the river, with wide windows that allow you to absorb the natural surrounds while also providing subtle natural lighting.

When it comes to dining, the Hoshinoya Kyoto boasts a Michelin-starred chef, the internationally traveled Ichiro Kubota, who fuses classic *kaiseki* with

Below One of the Hashizuku rooms, which have a bedroom downstairs and a lounge area upstairs with a lounger by the window for taking in the seasonally changing views.

Above A ryokan with a Michelin-starred chef. Expect the *kaiseki* to start with a platter as similarly artistic as this, and then be glad that the Hoshinoya's staff are able to explain all the incredible intricacies in English.

Right and below right
Reached via a short boat trip up the river from Arashiyama (although there is a walking route, too), guests are greeted by staff at the Hoshinoya's small boat landing, before being led to the main compound, by the tinkling sounds of the water garden, for a welcome drink. It's a process designed to ease one out of the modern day and into relaxation, and it works.

Below Many of the rooms at Hoshinoya directly overlook the river, whose soothing sounds lull you gently to sleep at night.

contemporary flair, with artistically arranged, multi-course seasonal menus (served in a private dining room or at a chef's counter) that might include a steamed wild mushroom curd with foie gras, abalone with a hint of *yuzu* citrus, or blue crab with a chrysanthemum sauce. A particular standout is the second-course *hassun* (appetizer platter), which features half a dozen morsels, and has the kind of presentation that makes you feel guilty about eating it, until the flavors take over. Making the complex meal accessible, there are near-fluent English-speaking staff who can talk you through each of the dishes and help with wine and local sake pairings.

Away from dining, guests can be further pampered with shiatsu and other spa treatments, and staff can arrange a variety of cultural experiences, including Zen meditation, flower arranging, and incense aromatherapy classes. The ryokan also organizes rickshaw rides around Arashiyama—an opportunity to take in the sights just like the aristocrats of old.

Hoshinoya Kyoto 星のや京都
Address: 11-2 Arashiyama Genrokuzancho, Nishikyo-ku, Kyoto 616-0007
Telephone: 050-3786-1144
Website: http://hoshinoyakyoto.jp/en
Email: info_kyoto@hoshinoya.com
Number of rooms: 25
Room rate: ¥¥¥¥

Right The Oku-no-Niwa by landscape artist Hiroki Hasegawa and Ueyakato Landscape. From the rooms, this looks like a Zen-inspired raked-sand garden, but it's actually fashioned from concrete, so you can walk over it and enjoy views from multiple angles.

Opposite page The library-slash-bar is designed on *kura* warehouse themes.

Above Another of the award-winning chef's creations. Try asking for a dinner seat at the counter to see the chefs at work. The dishes they produce are both visually stunning, and sublime to taste, and watching them being made adds to the experience.

Right Expect beds not futon and rooms that—although channeling Japanese sensibilities and with furnishings handcrafted by local artisans—are far more contemporary Western and Scandinavian in design.

In the natural surrounds of the Yunohana Onsen area, the Suisen blends the finest of ryokan and Western spa traditions. In the fall in particular, the mountain area is transformed by seasonal colors.

W estern spa meets ryokan at the Suisen, situated in the hot-spring–blessed countryside of Kameoka in western Kyoto Prefecture, an hour from central Kyoto. Out here, in the Yunohana Onsen area, it is said that warlords as far back as the Sengoku period (1467–1603) would come to bathe in the hot, soothing waters after battle. Who knows if that is fact or myth? But the Suisen's relationship with the area is more certain, and much more recent. Although

the Suisen can trace its roots back to the 1860s, when it opened as a lodging house in central Kyoto, it only relocated to Kameoka a generation ago, swapping city-center *machiya* for Western-influenced mountain retreat.

Now, the Suisen offers six types of guest rooms (thirteen rooms in all) with varying blends of East and West. The largest room, the giant Suisen suite, features a Western-style bedroom and living room (admittedly with busy designs that won't be a hit with anyone looking for Scandinavian simplicity), as well as a Japanese tatami room and an open-air bath made of *hinoki* cypress. The Japanese-style rooms are more attractive than the Western ones, with

more understated decor, even though they aren't all-out on tradition, as they also feature Western touches such as beds and decorative wallpaper.

In addition to in-room baths (which are set on the balcony in many rooms and have calming views out into the woods), the Suisen pampers with indoor and outdoor communal baths, as well as a bookable private open-air bath, crafted in stone and nestled among trees. Its water is drawn from the mineral-rich Yunohana Onsen source, its low-alkaline properties said to ease ailments ranging from strained muscles to gout. The Suisen has its own spa, too, Raran, which offers a range of Ayurvedic massages and treatments using

Left In some guest rooms the tatami almost merges with the outdoor wood decking, which provides views of a seasonally changing backdrop. Some rooms (like the Suisen suite) also have outdoor baths, allowing you to soak in the water and soak up nature at the same time.

Right Even in the rooms labeled Japanese, there is still a lot of Western design. **Below** Some rooms have their own outdoor hot-spring baths and there are two communal, gender-separated tubs, but the ultimate luxury is the Suisen's private outdoor bath.

Above The Suisen serves a classic welcome drink: a combination of matcha tea and *wagashi* (Japanese sweets).

medicinal herb oils, as well as shiatsu massages and foot and facial care.

While these kinds of spa treatments are not a traditional ryokan experience, dinner at Suisen is. Served in private dining rooms, the *kaiseki* courses make the most of abundant local produce, such as *matsutake* mushrooms in autumn, and *sansai* mountain vegetables in spring. The river offers sweet *ayu* fish, the fields local rice. Kameoka even has its own well-regarded sake makers.

Central Kyoto (which isn't difficult to access from Kameoka) is known for its array of historic and cultural sights—its geisha, temples and shrines, to call out just a few—but at the Suisen you are close to nature. From Kameoka, a popular activity is to boat down the Hozugawa River to Arashiyama (see page 112), a ninety-

Above In between dips in the private in-room bath you can cool down on your own patch of outdoor decking.

Left A ryokan breakfast is often a monumental affair and the Suisen is no exception. The range of pickles and small vegetable dishes, not to mention the light soup, grilled fish, rice, and other dishes, is a big start to the day, but one that's nutritionally balanced.

Right Aesthetically speaking, beds on tatami won't be to everyone's taste, but for anyone who can't manage on a futon (and it can be a struggle getting up and down if you have mobility issues) it makes a ryokan stay more accessible.

Below Dinner at the Suisen is served to you privately in your room, sometimes by the chef himself, and often features Western ingredients and dishes.

Right Between the main building and the private *rotemburo* bath (which guests can book for their own use), the Suisen has this patch of landscaped garden.

minute trip that takes in stunning gorges and the occasional white-water rapid. Another excursion option is the scenic Sagano Railway, which runs between Kameoka and Saga, with equally impressive rural views. Then again, you don't need to leave the Suisen to get a taste of nature, you just need to head for a bath.

Suisen 翠泉

Address: 6-3 Inoshiri, Ashinoyama, Hiedanocho, Kameoka, Kyoto 621-0034

Telephone: 0771-22-7575

Website: www.kyoto-suisen.com

Email: Via an online contact form

Number of rooms: 13

Room rate: ¥¥¥

SHIKITEI CENTRAL NARA

The spacious rooms at the Shikitei once formed part of humble temple accommodation but are now one of Nara's finest traditional inns, with a location in the heart of Nara's ancient sites.

The *kaiseki* cuisine is a feast on the eyes at the Shikitei, artistically arranged on local ceramic ware and employing local produce.

Built in 1899, the Shikitei initially functioned as simple temple lodgings known as *shukubo*, as is the case with many modern-day ryokan. But there can't be many other former *shukubo* that have ended up quite as fine as this one.

The decision to make the *shukubo* into a ryokan was taken in 1950, when Nara City was trying to increase the number of ryokan available for tourists. As a result, the Shikitei's thirty-two original rooms were reformed into eighteen. In the 1990s, after several more renovations, the current owner's father then created the current nine-room layout, a process that preserved the original outer structure and traditional feel while creating one of the most spacious ryokan around—one with a natural brightness that belies its age, and rooms that are more like suites, featuring high wood-paneled ceilings, light-toned wood beams, paper-screen doors, and calligraphic scrolls decorating the *tokonoma* alcove.

The details are everything at a ryokan; the small objects that catch your eye, the fleeting moments, the tiny touches you are not meant to notice, but which smooth the way. At the Shikitei, one of the most important touches comes at dinner, with a variety of *kaiseki* courses that take their inspiration from *chakaiseki* (meals served before a tea ceremony) and not only feature seasonal ingredients sourced from Nara Prefecture but are served in a selection of local *akahadayaki* pottery, which takes its name from its distinctive reddish finish (*akahada* literally means "red skin"). This pottery has a milky white glaze that's often coupled with *narae*, a kind of unrefined

Above Rooms come with small cubby holes like this next to the main tatami area—spots where you can look out at nature, but also look inward to enjoy the design and style of the room.
Below The communal bath is made of cypress, which gives off a lovely gentle aroma as you soak.

Right There are no rooms at the Shikitei that disappoint. All are spacious and with brightness and freshness that belies their age. This one even has its own dry landscaped garden—not for walking on, just looking at.

Right The small garden by the entrance has a lovely carpeting of moss. For more greenery, you are only a few minutes on foot from Nara Park, a vast swathe of green inhabited by semi-tame deer.

decoration based on sutras or Buddhist lotus patterns designed to bring out the simplicity of the pottery's surface. As with many fine ryokan, it's not just the quality and look of the *kaiseki* that matters, it's the quality, aesthetics, and even the history of the dishes in which it is served.

The communal Furouyu bathhouse is a modest affair compared to the baths in bathing-focused hot-spring resorts like Atami and Hakone, but this is typical of bathhouses found in Nara and Kyoto. At the Shikitei, however, a bathtub made of aromatic Japanese cypress is a luxurious touch. A greater luxury is the tatami matting that covers not just guest room floors, but also the hallways and other communal areas throughout the ryokan, allowing guests the unusual and freeing experience of walking around barefoot for

the duration of their stay. There's also a traditional green tea and sweet service upon arrival—a mini tea ceremony of sorts—that's held in the first-floor Seikouan tea room. The Shikitei also has plenty of Buddhist art on display, from the three calligraphic scrolls in the entrance area bearing auspicious Chinese characters written three generations earlier by the head priest of the historic Kofukuji Temple, to scrolls written by the former Elder of Todaiji Temple and, in the small garden, sculptures by artist Koumei Takeda.

The Shikitei's location on the edge of Nara Park means it is a stroll away from several of Japan's most famous religious sites. Closest at hand is the seventh-century Kofukuji Temple, which is known for its six-hundred-year-old five-story pagoda. The temple is also home to a collection of

Buddhist statues that includes one of Japan's most famous relics, a standing statue of the three-headed, six-armed Ashura, said to date to the 730s. Other parts of the park are the sites of Todaiji Temple and Kasuga Grand Shrine (see page 128 for more information), which, like Kofukuji, are both designated UNESCO World Heritage sites.

Shikitei 四季亭
Address: 1163 Takabatakecho, Nara City, Nara 630-8301
Telephone: 0742-22-5531
Website: www.shikitei.co.jp
Email: info@shikitei.co.jp
Number of rooms: 9
Room rate: ¥¥¥¥

Connected to a Western-style hotel popular with tourists, the Wakasa is a very foreigner-friendly and relatively new ryokan. Built in a traditional style, it also gives access to some of Japan's most unforgettable heritage sites.

Staff serve a classic local flavor at breakfast. *Cha-gayu* is a nourishing porridge made with rice and tea.

W hile Kyoto has a slew of historic ryokan and townhouses, Nara is far from awash in traditional accommodation—something of an oddity given that Nara is the most venerable of Japanese cities. It was the country's capital from 710–794, and is often referred to as "the birthplace of Japanese civilization". It was to help address that oddity that the Wakasa Bettei was created in 2014.

The Wakasa (and this might be the only letdown of sorts) is entered through its older Western-style sister hotel rather than through a traditional ryokan lobby, but from thereon, the Wakasa is all tradition. Inspired by Nara's old *machiya* townhouses —the kind that still define the Naramachi area south of Nara's Kintetsu Station—

designer Yoshikazu Nagai has incorporated features such as latticed wooden doors, square (not the typical rectangular) tatami mats in guest rooms, and various Nara craft touches: *sarashi* cloth used for doorway curtains, table runners and small accessories; and strings of woven good luck charms hanging outside guest room doors. The ryokan is new, but its design is rooted in rich Nara traditions.

When it comes to dining, meals are taken in the first-floor dining hall, which features several private cubbies and more of the old townhouse design. Like the interiors, the meals too celebrate the past. Dinner is multi-course *kaiseki*, centered on seasonal produce and high-grade seafood brought in daily from the markets of Osaka, and served with local touches like pungent *narazuke* pickles, or eggplant preserved in sake lees. Another local flavor comes at breakfast, with Nara tea gruel, which is made with roasted green tea and topped with your choice of dried fish, seaweed, or sesame seeds, served alongside grilled fish and other common ryokan morning fare.

For bathing, each of the mostly compact rooms (they vary from 160 to 340 square feet [15 to 32 square meters]) has its own small bath—some ceramic, some cedar wood, some set outside, but all using normal, not hot-spring water. On the top floor is a communal bathtub with panoramic views out toward Mount Wakakusa and the roof of the Great Hall at Todaiji Temple, and a skylight that at night allows you to bathe under the stars.

The Wakasa also has location on its side, being just a short walk from one of Japan's most lauded temples, the eighth-century Todaiji and its great Daibutsu-den hall, which houses a magnificent 1,400-year-old, 50-foot (15-meter) tall bronze statue of Buddha. From there, as the Wakasa's English-speaking staff are happy to explain, guests can embark on a several-hour walk that takes in most of Nara's main historic sites; many, like Todaiji, are designated UNESCO World Heritage sites. That includes the seventh-century Kofukuji, and the eighth-century Kasuga Grand Shrine, which is defined by a stone lantern-lined approach leading to a

At dinner, the sashimi platter is one of the highlights. The Wakasa Bettei brings it in daily from the seafood market in Osaka, Japan's second city, nineteen miles (thirty kilometers) away.

Left The rooms at the Wakasa are modern built, but fully traditional in design, and also come with small outdoor baths.

Below The deer get almost everywhere in Nara, and especially so in the Wakasa, where they appear as motifs and stuffed toys.

main shrine building adorned by several thousand bronze lanterns. And, of course, there's Nara Park, around which these sights are scattered, and which is known for its fairly tame deer, which in turn explains one of the Wakasa's regularly occurring motifs—look for the stuffed toy deer in common areas, silver deer pins worn by the manager, and you may even spot deer-shaped fittings in the rooms.

Wakasa Bettei 和鹿彩別邸

Address: 1 Higashimichi, Kita-Handa, Nara City, Nara 630-8274

Telephone: 0742-23-5858

Website: http://wakasa-bettei.com

Email: n-wakasa@syd.odn.ne.jp

Number of rooms: 11

Room rate: ¥¥¥

Right The main hall of Todaiji Temple is one of several UNESCO World Heritage sights within easy walking distance of the Wakasa Bettei. The giant Buddha statue inside is one of Japan's great sights, but so too is the much less heralded sunset from the Niqatsudo Hall next to Todaiji.

You wouldn't know it from the calm of the Senjuan, but Minakami is an adrenalin junkie's paradise for its white-water rafting and other outdoor pursuits. Like yin and yang, the Senjuan is an entirely different affair—a modern-day ryokan in the finest sense of the term.

Above The thatched entrance is so discreet you could easily pass by and never realize that beyond lies something quite like the Senjuan.

Set at the foot of Mount Tanigawa, which straddles the border of Gunma and Niigata Prefectures a couple of hours to the north of Tokyo, the Senjuan bills itself as a "modern Japanese-style inn", combining contemporary and traditional design elements to create a plush retreat that has been awarded with membership of the exclusive Relais & Chateaux group of independently owned luxury hotels.

Take a walk around the common areas and you will notice that the Senjuan certainly has many features that mark it as different to the norm: a curved twenty-six-foot- (eight-meter-) high corridor with floor-to-ceiling windows that reveal natural scenery; Kyoto-style clay walls that in places are decorated with dark Edo-style ink; sliding doors featuring intricate *kumiko* wood joinery; and *washi* paper accents here and there.

The rooms are appointed in classic ryokan style, with ikebana arrangements in the *tokonoma* alcove and low rectangular table on tatami-mat flooring. There are two Japanese-Western rooms with wood floors, as well as a Western-style room that has a patterned marble floor. Other rooms have distinguishing touches such as wood decking that extends into the surrounding foliage, and rustic clay walls with swirling

Right Large picture windows providing expansive views of the surrounding countryside are a signature feature of this ryokan.

Opposite page, bottom One of the private dining spaces. Some people prefer in-room dining, partly because once dinner is done you can roll away from the table and pass out on the tatami, but there's something special about "going out" for dinner, especially when you get views like this.

Below The "Special SP" room. Many apartments in Japan aren't this spacious, and they certainly wouldn't have the open-air bath surrounded by greenery that this room boasts.

Right The "Japanese S" room. The table design is striking, and this room also has its own large semi-outdoor bath and a lovely bit of wood decking for relaxing in the fresh air.

patterns. All rooms have their own open-air baths, with views into the dense woodlands that covers Mount Tanigawa, but there are also a pair of large communal baths available—the outdoor Hotaru-no-Yu, a stone bath looking into lush woods, and Uchi-yu, an aromatic indoor wooden bath. Both of these communal baths, like the in-room baths, use natural, mineral-rich hot-spring water. The Senjuan

Above Bathing is an important part of the experience at most ryokan, but especially so at the Senjuan. To go with the range of plush in-room baths, there are several communal options, including this indoor affair.

Left As well as bathing, relaxation options at the Senjuan include spa treatments at the Sora beauty salon that range from facials to full-body massages.

Above left The entrance to the Nagara-chaya restaurant, where all meals at the Senjuan are served in private spaces.
Below left Slide back the bathroom door to step into your own private hot-spring bath.

Above The Hotaru no Yu communal bath. Hotaru is the Japanese word for firefly, which mate in May and are active in June in Japan, just before summer starts to get hot and sticky. If you are lucky, you never know, you might get to see some from the bath that takes their name. The other outdoor communal bath is named Suzumushi—bell cricket.

The Minakami area, where the Senjuan is located, has a reputation as an adventure playground, with numerous companies offering activities such as white-water rafting and canyoning. There are well-rated ski resorts and golf courses in the area, too; all providing an active counterpoint to the calm and relaxation of the Senjuan.

provides additional pampering at its Sora spa, which offers full-body massages, facial treatments, anti-freckle treatments, and a dozen or so other beauty options.

Then there is the food. Meals at the Senjuan are served in private spaces in the Nagara-chaya dining room—where some of the tables have *horigotatsu* sunken seating. For the morning meal guests can choose either traditional Japanese-style fare—rice, pickles, grilled fish and the like—or a continental-style breakfast. Dinner is an elaborate *kaiseki* affair, featuring seasonal, local produce that can be paired with an extensive selection of sake, wines, and *shochu* (a clear distilled spirit made from rice, barley, sweet potato, or black sugar).

Bettei Senjuan 仙寿庵
Address: 614 Tanigawa, Minakami-machi, Tone, Gunma 379-1619
Telephone: 0278-72-2469
Website: www.senjyuan.jp
Email: info@senjyuan.jp
Number of rooms: 18
Room rate: ¥¥¥¥

The lobby at the Ryugon is one of the most charming and rustic you'll find, with its aged woods, the gentle aroma from the *irori* sunken hearths, and, if you were to look up here, its high-vaulted ceiling.

Left The exterior of this former samurai's residence screams history, hinting at what's to come inside.

Below The communal areas—like the lobby—still feel like someone lives here, what with touches such as the open hearth and the traditional *tansu* chest of drawers, not to mention ornaments that could have been in the family for centuries. It's rustic and homely; the kind of place you can relax into with ease.

In addition to these eleven rooms, there are seven further rooms that feature *irori* hearths, around which part of the evening meal can be cooked. The main hall also has two partitioned rooms for large groups, and there's a newer annex in the garden, built in 1996, that's home to four pond-side rooms.

Whichever room one opts for, dining at the Ryugon is an in-room affair that revolves around local specialties. Breakfast utilizes highly prized *koshihikari* rice from Minami-Uonuma that's served alongside dishes such as miso soup, char-grilled dried fish, or *tomaru* eggs from chickens

A former samurai residence, transformed into a ryokan. A night at the Ryugon is a night in old Japan, the 240-year-old building an enchanting mix of creaking wooden corridors, high-vaulted ceilings, beautiful gardens, and Buddhist decorations.

The eleven standard rooms exude an old, almost temple-like charm. The wooden fixtures and fittings have darkened with age. The *tokonoma* alcoves are adorned simply with calligraphic scrolls written by the former abbot of the local Untoan Temple, whose predecessor many generations prior is said to have suggested the name Ryugon (after a temple of the same name) to the inn's original owners. And from the windows one can enjoy views of a sprawling garden, that changes its tone along with the changing of the seasons, from the deep pinks and purples of plum blossom in early spring through to a thick carpet of white in midwinter.

Left In the rooms in winter, you'll often find a *kotatsu*—a heated table to put your legs under.
Below The Ryugon's *okami* ("house mother") kneels to welcome guests. The calligraphy behind her is a feature in the rooms. Much of it was written by the former abbot of a nearby temple.

fed on local rice. Depending on the season, the *kaiseki* dinner might include *tomaru* chicken as part of a hearty hot pot, while other distinctly Niigata dishes on the multi-course menu might be *noppe* vegetable soup, river-fish sashimi, edible wild plants, or grilled *ayu* sweet fish.

The Ryugon has a selection of communal baths, each with its own distinctive features. The Waraku-no-Yu bathhouse, which is divided into baths for men and women, has its roof held aloft by rustic uncut timber columns, under which the rocky pool feels almost connected to the garden. The Madoka-no Yu, a one-story, gender-separated bathhouse with mortar walls and sloping timber

ceiling, catches garden reflections in its waters. There are two other smaller baths—for private use only—that are enshrouded by woods.

For guests desiring a deeper cultural experience, the Ryugon provides a variety of activities and events. Year round, in a throwback to a time before TV and radio, there are nightly storytelling sessions. In the autumn guests may be offered the chance to make *mochi* rice cakes, an entertaining process that involves pounding rice with a large wooden mallet to create a dough. For an additional charge, the ryokan can also arrange traditional *tsugaru-shamisen* (a three-stringed instrument) performances and lessons, and

taiko drumming shows and workshops. There is also the option of trying the tea ceremony; learning how to hold the cup correctly, how to turn it, when to sip, and many of the other subtle nuances of this quintessentially Japanese art form.

Ryugon 龍言
Address: 79 Sakadoyamagiwa, Minami-Uonoma, Niigata 949-6611
Telephone: 025-772-3470
Website: www.ryugon.co.jp
Email: info@ryugon.co.jp
Number of rooms: 25
Room rate: ¥¥¥

One of the first super sleek ryokan to fuse Japanese aesthetics and hospitality with resort sensibilities, the Hoshinoya Karuizawa is already established as a modern-day classic with a recipe that has since been tweaked to great effect elsewhere in Japan by Hoshino Resorts.

Karuizawa in Nagano Prefecture—eighty minutes by bullet train from Tokyo—is one of Japan's classic holiday retreats, where the mild summers and winter snowfall have long attracted Japan's well-heeled, who come here to their holiday villas for weekends of tennis, golf, and skiing. To give just one example of the area's status, it was on a Karuizawa tennis court that the current emperor and empress first met in the 1950s. And it's here, nestled in a forest-covered valley through which a river gently flows, where you'll find the Hoshinoya Karuizawa, a "highland resort village" with guest pavilions blended into the natural environment.

The pavilions have all been designed with a floor-level perspective, the living rooms featuring low tables and sofas to increase the feeling of ceiling height and enhance the room's sense of spaciousness. Large windows and wide terraces provide either river or forested mountain views. There are aromatic cedar bathtubs, positioned indoors but with scenic views.

Unlike a traditional ryokan, the Hoshinoya Karuizawa offers a variety of dining options. At the main restaurant, Kasuke, head chef Eiji Inake crafts refined "nouveau natural cuisine", a variation on classic *kaiseki* that employs fresh, seasonal, local produce to create a succession of dishes designed to stimulate sight, scent, and taste. Kasuke also serves a beef

shabu-shabu course. Just off the premises, the Hoshinoya-run Bleston Court Yukawatan serves French cuisine. There are also two casual dining options nearby, the Shomin Shokudo and the Harunire Terrace, whose menus feature noodles, pizza, and other fare that goes well with a beer or two.

As a resort, the Hoshinoya teams up with local companies to offer a variety of activities and experiences not usually offered by a ryokan, such as guided nature walks and horse trekking. Guests can also indulge in pampering at the Hoshinoya's own spa, which offers a range of massage and aromatherapy treatments, or visit the airy teahouse in the woods for morning breathing exercises. Less energetic guests might enjoy simply relaxing in the library.

Above and left The Hoshinoya is one of the most stunning ryokan in Japan—a totally modern resort with a variety of restaurants that updates the ryokan traditions.

Or there are the baths. The Tombo-no-yu bathhouse has an indoor stone bath built into cedar flooring, and a large open-air bath, both with soothing low-alkaline waters. There is also a sauna.

Away from the Hoshinoya, Karuizawa has plenty of other things worth checking out. Go for a spot of retail therapy at the sprawling Karuizawa Prince Shopping Plaza near JR Karuizawa Station's south exit, which is home to dozens of outlet stores for well-known fashion and sports brands. North of the station, the road leads to the Kyu-Karuizawa area, which is worth a stroll to check out the delicatessens (ham, sausages and cheese are local specialties),

Above There is a range of dining options at the Hoshinoya, but as the saying goes, when in Rome, do as the Romans do. The unmissable take on *kaiseki* here—a kind of nouveau cuisine, *kaiseki* fusion—is exceptional in every regard, from initial visual impact through to taste.

Right For bathing, the Hoshinoya incorporates a hot spring—the Tombo-no-Yu—that has been here since the 1910s, long before the Hoshinoya was built on the site. There is also a Meditation Bath that combines one stark but brightly lit area and an entirely blacked-out area.

cafés, casual eateries, souvenir stores, and historic sites like Karuizwa's old catholic church and the Shaw Memorial Chapel—reminders of the foreign influences that helped shape Karuizawa.

Hoshinoya Karuizawa 星のや軽井沢
Address: Hoshino, Karuizawa, Kitasaku, Nagano 389-0194
Telephone: 050-3786-1144
Website: http://hoshinoyakaruizawa.com/en
Email: info@hoshinoya.com
Number of rooms: 77
Room rate: ¥¥¥

The pine-accented garden at the Houshi dates to the 1600s, but that's just a fraction of this ryokan's story. This second-oldest ryokan in Japan—though it predates the word ryokan by centuries—traces its first incarnation to the 700s.

When the Houshi advertises "1,300 years of history", it isn't a typo. Located in the Awazu Onsen area of Ishikawa Prefecture, the Houshi is the second-oldest hotel in the world, founded in 718 by Buddhist monk Garyo Houshi as a therapeutic retreat. Even more remarkably, it's been run by the same family since it opened forty-six generations ago. There are royal families that can't trace their lineage back that far.

The current wood-made building isn't from the 700s, but parts of the Houshi are centuries old. The moss-tinged pine garden is believed to date back to the 1600s, and is thought to have been designed and constructed by famed garden landscaper Kobori Enshu, who created the gardens at historic sites such as the Sento Imperial Palace and Katsura Villa in Kyoto.

Each room has a view of the garden, and incorporates classic ryokan features: gently scented tatami matting on which futon are put down at night, a *tokonoma* alcove accented by hanging scrolls and flower arrangements, sliding paper screen doors, and (in most rooms) naturally colored plastered walls. The only departure from this traditional style is in the Enmeikaku (meaning "long-life pavilion"), a villa for VIPs that is found deep in the garden, where the room walls are painted an auspicious red and there are distinctly non-Japanese touches such as Persian rugs.

Both dinner—which is classic *kaiseki*—and breakfast are served in the guests' room at a low table by kimono-clad staff, who bring in a succession of small dishes that feature fresh local seafood and seasonal produce. Highlighting some of Ishikawa's traditional crafts, dishes might arrive on Yamanaka lacquerware, which has been made in the Yamanaka Onsen area just to the south of Awazu since the 1800s, or the older and more decorative Kutani-yaki porcelain, which is distinguished by its use of greens, yellows, reds, purples, and navy blues.

When it's time for bathing, the Houshi has both in-room bathrooms and a choice of five public hot-springs: two gender-separated indoor baths and two gender-separated outdoor baths, each of which is made from a mix of marble and rock. There

Above Enjoy a tea-ceremony-style welcome drink, one of many forays into traditional culture at the Houshi.

Below The guest rooms are classically designed, all except the Enmeikaku for VIPs, which features red walls and decorative rugs—quite a contrast to the rest of the ryokan's minimalist decor. Even the *tokonoma* is more richly decorated than normal, with multiple scrolls and freshly made ikebana.

Rooms at the Houshi are complete with many classic ryokan design features, from tatami-mat floors to paper screen doors, and each room also has views of the historic garden.

One wonders what Basho would have written about the Houshi. After all, it would be the perfect place to sit peacefully and compose a haiku.

Houshi 法師
Address: Awazu Onsen, Komatsu, Ishikawa 923-0326
Telephone: 0761-65-1111
Website: www.ho-shi.co.jp
Email: ho-shi@ho-shi.co.jp
Number of rooms: 74
Room rate: ¥

is also one smaller bath that can be rented privately—ideal if you are a bit too shy to get naked with everyone else, even though the communal baths really shouldn't be missed.

Neither should the sights of the Awazu Onsen area. A couple of miles south, the mountain-side Nata Temple is even older than the Houshi, having first been built in 717, although the current buildings are now mostly from the 1600s. These include a three-story wooden pagoda that like the rest of the temple complex is enshrouded by cedar trees and punctuated by strange natural rock formations that are said to have inspired the legendary haiku poet Matsuo Basho to pen the following poem: "The autumn wind is whiter than the white cliffs of the stony mountain".

The five hot-spring baths at the Houshi include two gender-separated outdoor baths immersed in greenery. For anyone too shy to use a communal bath, there's also one private bath that can be rented.

The Araya's Ochin-no-Ma stateroom showcases local crafts and traditions, employing regional specialties such as lacquering on the columns and rich vermilion-colored walls to create a regal atmosphere.

Left Slip off your shoes and enter a world steeped in tradition.
Right Winter sees this part of Japan carpeted in white.
Opposite below Some rooms have their own open-air baths, but everybody has access to the three communal bathhouses, including the cypress-scented Ruriko indoor bath.

Bathing and crafts. The Yamashiro Onsen area in the Kaga region of Ishikawa Prefecture has long been indelibly linked to both. As far back as 1,300 years ago, hot-spring bathing has been recorded here, while the local Kutani-yaki porcelain has thrived for centuries, so it's probably no surprise that the area's finest ryokan—the Araya Totoan—celebrates both.

The communal baths at the Araya Totoan are a definite highlight, in particular the Ruriko, which has a scented cypress bath with lightly colored wooden walls and ceilings. The Yamashiro Onsen source, which is relatively shallow compared to other hot springs, arrives at a piping-hot 64 degrees Celsius (147 degrees Farenheit), although it is cooler when piped into the baths. It has properties that soothe back pain, neuralgia, skin conditions, and other ailments. When drunk—not directly from the baths, obviously—the water is believed to be beneficial for people with diabetes, hypertension, and stomach issues. More importantly, soaking in the water just feels good.

Five of the rooms at the Araya—suite-like in size—also have their own open-air baths. The Wakana room has a cypress bath tub in a wood-paneled room offering a window-framed glimpse of the Araya's garden. Its tatami-matted main room opens on to a terrace and there is a separate bedroom with a low bed. There are also eleven humbler guest rooms (although humble at the Araya is still plush) featuring tatami flooring and dim, natural lighting that allows shadows to decorate the plaster walls. In addition, there's one grand stateroom—the Ochin-no-Ma—that features lacquer-coated columns and striking vermilion-colored walls that are distinctive to the Kaga area of Ishikawa, recalling the aristocratic style of the Maeda clan that once ruled this domain.

Many rooms come with garden views. The Araya Totoan's garden was created in the early seventeenth century and is in the *yamakuro-chisen-shiki* style, featuring fieldstones and stately trees that have been brought in from across Japan, and flora and foliage that transforms itself seasonally. Hidden within it is the wooden Arisugawa-sanso cottage, built for an Imperial visit in the late 1800s and now functioning as a bar with a wide range of wines.

exhibitions and opportunities to make and glaze pottery. Another local attraction is the Edo-style Soyu and Meiji-style Ko-Soyu public baths in the center of town, where you can sample some more of the area's bathing history—the latter even has Kutani-yaki wall tiles.

Araya Totoan あらや滔々庵
Address: Yamashiro Onsen, Kaga, Ishikawa 922-0242
Telephone: 0120-26-3939
Website: www.araya-totoan.com
Email: info@araya-totoan.com
Number of rooms: 18
Room rate: ¥¥¥

Above The Araya's intricate meals are served on nationally renowned local crafts, such as Kutani-yaki porcelain and Yamanaka lacquerware. The ryokan can also arrange for guests to visit kilns and workshops in the area.

The Araya also enjoys connections to the arts. Noted artist and epicure Kitaoji Rosanjin (1883–1959) stayed in the Yamashiro area for a year in the early 1900s, studying the region's ceramic and lacquerware crafts, and some of his earliest works were commissioned by ryokan in the area. The Araya Totoan was no exception, and today it displays Rosanjin work that includes a decorative red plate and screen paintings. At dinner time the multi-course *kaiseki* is served on replicas of Rosanjin's acclaimed ceramics as well as on Kutani-yaki porcelain and Yamanaka lacquerware crafted by local artisans.

One of the highlights of a trip to the Yamashiro Onsen area is the chance to visit the Kutaniyaki Kiln Exhibition Pavilion, home to a working kiln as well as

The style of the *tokonoma* alcove in this guest room encapsulates the overall feel of the Kayotei Inn. Uncluttered, simple, and smart, it gets the balance between tradition and contemporary just right.

Situated in the peace and quiet of Yamanaka Onsen, a small hot-spring town in Ishikawa Prefecture, the Kayotei Inn is an intriguing blend of old and new; a traditional ryokan that celebrates local artisans but isn't afraid to mix tradition with contemporary sensibilities.

The mix of styles is evident as soon as you step inside; hardwood and tatami-matted floors combine with subtly placed wood carvings, modern sculptures, and antique furnishings. The ten guest rooms have traditional design elements such as tatami flooring, paper screen doors, low tables of aged oak, wood-paneled ceilings, decorative calligraphic wall hangings, and minimalist ikebana flower arrangements, all accented with local Yamanaka lacquerware and ceramics. Two of the rooms, however, provide a slight departure from tradition by offering beds instead of futon, while three others deliver additional luxury with their own open-air baths—two of which are wooden, one of which is made of stone—that boast views into dense mountainside woods.

It is said that the Buddhist monk Gyoki—the man recognized as the founder of mapping in Japan—discovered Yamanaka's hot springs and their supposed healing powers in the 700s, and since then Yamanaka and hot-spring bathing have become synonymous with one another. The Kayotei honors that hot-spring connection with both in-room baths and a large communal bath featuring giant glass windows that that give a sense of being enshrouded by forest.

Local is a major theme at the Kayotei, and as well as crafts and bathing, regional flavors are also highlighted here. Served in private tatami-mat dining rooms, the evening *kaiseki* will include local seafood, locally made tofu, freshly caught river fish, and locally grown seasonal vegetables, all of which the chefs will use to create an array of artistically arranged, subtly flavored dishes that will often be served on Yamanaka lacquerware.

Below The entrance area (right), where one leaves one's shoes for the duration of the stay, and the guest rooms (left) ooze tradition, but with both a modern edge, thanks to touches like the polished woodwork, and an old European vibe from the occasional bit of antique furniture.

Guests can enjoy fresh air and wooded mountainside and riverside trails en route to the pretty Kakusenkei Gorge, the rugged beauty of which is a major reason (along with the hot-spring bathing) that the famous wandering haiku poet Matsuo Basho ranked Yamanaka as one of Japan's top three hot-spring areas; it was here that he wrote (admittedly, not his most stunning poem when read in English) "Here / the joy / of a good walk" while nearing the end of the travels that would later become the classic poem-infused travelogue *The Narrow Road to the Deep North*, a must-read for those with an interest in old Japan. You can also learn more about the area's lacquerware with a visit to the Yamanaka Lacquerware Traditional Industry Museum or any of the craft workshops in the town; something the staff at the Kayotei are happy to arrange.

Kayotei Inn かよう亭

Address: 1-20 Higashimachi, Yamanaka Onsen, Ishikawa 922-0114
Telephone: 0761-78-1410
Website: www.kayotei.jp
Email: kayotei@fork.ocn.ne.jp
Number of rooms: 10
Room rate: ¥¥¥¥

Above Even if you have one of the guest rooms with a private open-air bath, you have to try Kayotei's communal bath. It's indoors, but its floor-to-ceiling windows give a sense of bathing in the forest.
Below Dinner at the Kayotei is multi-course *kaiseki* served in private rooms and featuring local produce as well as super-fresh seafood from the Sea of Japan.

WA-NO-SATO MIYA MURA, GIFU

The Wa-no-Sato immerses visitors in traditional rural Japan, its centuries-old farmhouses providing a very different atmosphere from a typical ryokan, even though it also delivers all the best ryokan elements—hospitality, fine cuisine, relaxation, and tranquility.

dyllic. Quaint. Rustic. The Wa-no-Sato comes from a very different time, bringing with it the kind of look that could have come straight from a fairytale. Its collection of thatched, earthen-walled buildings have found the perfect home alongside a babbling river that's buried deep in wooded mountainside, after being relocated from other parts of Gifu Prefecture in the early 1990s and carefully restored to function as a ryokan.

The Wa-no-Sato comprises a main building with four guest rooms plus four separate private 100- to 160-year-old farmhouse villas that are built in the striking *gassho-zukuri* style, a name that translates as "praying hands", a reference to the sharply angled thatched roofs, which are designed to prevent heavy snowfall from accumulating on top of the building and damaging it.

Inside the buildings there are slats high in the ceiling to provide natural ventilation, and to allow smoke from the fires that would have once lit the center of the rooms to escape. These fires would have served multiple purposes; to heat, to cook, to dry the thatching, to see off bugs and insects. Things are a bit more refined at the Wa-no-Sato. There are still small hearths in places and rough earthen walls, but also smart tatami and wood flooring, large windows with views into the wooded surrounds, and many classic ryokan design elements.

The main building at first glance appears traditional, with a large open-hearth in the lobby scenting the air as smoke drifts high into the dark vaulted roof space. The four rooms in this main building follow a more refined ryokan style, with tatami, screen doors, and a low table, combined with one or two unexpected touches. One room has a small open-hearth for heating a cast-iron kettle. Three of the rooms have terraces with views out into nature. They all have heated *kotatsu* tables that guests can huddle around in winter.

All the guest rooms have their own aromatic cypress baths that are ideal for keeping out the cold and unwinding, but it's better to head for one of the two communal tubs—there's a cypress bath and a rocky bath—as both of these draw on natural hot-spring water and have views into the woods.

Come dinner time, the *kaiseki* here is centered around local produce such as *sansai* mountain vegetables, river fish, and highly prized Hida beef, which might be seared on a hot stone or be the star ingredient in a *sukiyaki*, while the presentation includes natural touches that match the rustic locale, using a varied mix of ceramic, lacquerware, and porcelain dishes accented perhaps by a sprig of blossom in spring or earth-toned leaves in the autumn.

Above Inside one of the four private farmhouse villas. You can see how the roof slopes extremely steeply to prevent snow accumulating in winter—a distinctive regional style called *gassho-zukuri* (hands-in-prayer style).

Left Staying at the Wa-no-Sato's small collection of historic farmhouses is like being transported back to an old hamlet—peaceful and idyllic, perfect for enjoying a break in nature.

In the local area, there is lots to see and do. The Hida Folk Village is a worthwhile stop to learn more about *gassho-zukuri* and other regional traditions, being home to more than thirty historic buildings that house folk materials and crafts, and host regular demonstrations of and workshops on crafts such as *sashiko* quilting, Hida lacquer-working, and dyeing. Further afield, for guests with a car, there's the unmissable Shirakawa-go village, a UNESCO World Heritage-designated site at the foot of Mount Haku-san that is arguably one of Japan's most scenic spots; a vista of rice fields and mountain scenery punctuated by more than a hundred thatched *gassho-zukuri* houses. Visiting Shirakawa-go is a journey back in time, much like a night at the Wa-no-Sato.

Above The lobby of the main building, which houses four guest rooms. The open hearth—called an *irori*—helps to warm and gives off a gentle, welcoming aroma. It's also used to cook on.
Left Each room and farmhouse has its own cypress bath, but there are two large communal tubs, too. This one is made of aromatic wood, the other of rock.

Wa-no-Sato 和乃里
Address: 1682 Ichinomiya-cho, Takayama, Gifu 509-3505
Telephone: 0577-53-2321

Website: www.wanosato.com
Email: info@www.wanosato.com
Number of rooms: 8
Room rate: ¥¥¥¥

The lobby and other communal areas at the Nishimuraya look
onto an ornate inner garden—one of many traditional
touches that make the ryokan one of the finest in the region.

Above The entrance shows the three kanji for Nishimuraya, literally "west village home".

Below Like all the best ryokan, seasonal is a key word when it comes to dining at the Nishimuraya, with winter seeing some of Japan's finest crab on the menu.

Right A small garden nestled between the rooms. It's a defining feature at many ryokan to glimpse a variety of small scenes like this as one walks around the property.

You know a ryokan is historic when it has its own museum. In the 150 years since the Nishimuraya first opened in the hot-spring–rich Kinosaki Onsen, it has certainly put together an extensive collection, its two-floor museum displaying an array of photography, art, and artefacts—from ceramics to armory—that help document Nishimuraya's and parts of Japan's history.

Even away from the museum, the past is still present here. The thirty rooms in the main building and the four in the 1960s-built Hiratakan annex—designed in the teahouse-inspired *sukiya* style by master architect Masaya Hirata—ooze old charm, being defined by tatami matting, simple plaster walls, wooden ceilings, and sliding paper-screen doors that in the annex open to reveal a pretty courtyard garden. Other rooms have views of traditional landscaping that blends tall pines and sculpted bushes, mossy stone statues, and carp ponds. For guests after extra privacy and seclusion, two rooms—Asuka and Hatsune—also boast terraces that connect to private gardens and open-air baths.

Food—seasonally changing *kaiseki*—is another major highlight. In spring, when the Nishimuraya's garden is dappled by the pinks of cherry blossoms, head chef Etsunobu Takahashi works seasonal ingredients like bamboo shoot and firefly squid into the intricate multi-course feast, such as abalone and *ayu* sweetfish in summer. During crab season from November through March, when the

Nishimuraya sources highly prized *matsuba-gani* from the local ports of Tsuiyama and Shibayama, the *kaiseki* refocuses with crab served as sashimi, boiled, grilled, and in hot pots; and not just the succulent white flesh—the *kani miso* (crab innards) is a particular delicacy. And year-round, there's always the opportunity to try Tajima beef, too.

Kinosaki Onsen's reputation as a hot-spring area goes back to the Nara era (710–784), and the seven public baths in Kinosaki still form the town's central attraction, people turning back time and leaving their ryokan in their cotton *yukata* gowns to stroll between the bathhouses, all of which are within a fifteen-minute walk of the Nishimuraya and free to enter for Nishimuraya guests. All baths have their own distinctive characteristics: the Gosho-no-Yu, for example, has an outdoor bath facing a waterfall, while the Sato-no-Yu bathhouse mixes outdoor bathing with a selection of saunas.

Of course, the Nishimuraya has a fine selection of baths itself. Its Kichi-no-Yu bathhouse, which combines a large indoor bath and an outdoor bath set in a grove of bamboo, is scented with the delicate aroma of cypress. The Fuku-no-Yu baths are quite

Right One of many bathing options, the Kichi-no-Yu mixes indoor and outdoor tubs, plus a small bamboo grove.
Below The archetypal ryokan room, with classic elements such as paper screen doors, tatami, and a low table. But there are some twists—note the painting in the *tokonoma* alcove, not a scroll, and bonsai instead of ikebana.

a departure in style, with round, tiled tubs, patterned tiles on the walls, and even rounded doorways that could have come straight from Hobbiton. Then there's the indoor Shou-no-Yu bath, which through large windows looks into the Hiratakan's courtyard garden. One thing that's certain when you stay at the Nishimuraya—there's no shortage of great bathing opportunities.

Nishimuraya Honkan 西村屋本館
Address: 469 Yushima Kinosaki, Toyooka, Hyogo 669-6101
Telephone: 0796-32-2211
Website: http://nishimuraya.ne.jp
Email: honkan@nishimuraya.ne.jp
Number of rooms: 34
Room rate: ¥¥¥

Tosen Goshobo is one of Japan's most historic ryokan. Since its first incarnation eight hundred years ago, it has welcomed VIPs from shoguns to renowned novelists.

Above Staff test the waters. At first, the best hot-spring baths feel too hot to the toe, but after you gradually slip in and you become accustomed to the heat, a deeply soothing sensation takes over, relaxing both muscles and mind.
Right While bathing, guests also get to take in garden views.
Below Meals are exquisite, as you'd expect of a top ryokan, but the Tosen offers a no-meal plan if you book one of the standard Chikyu rooms, a great way to experience this level of accommodation without breaking the bank.

Established in 1191, Tosen Goshobo drips history, over the years having hosted some of Japan's most famous shogun, spiritual leaders, and literati. To put its age into some international perspective, in the 1190s England's King Richard, "The Lion Heart", was off crusading against the armies of Saladin. In the king's absences, Robin Hood and his merry men were (in fiction, anyway) robbing the rich to give to the poor. Back in Japan, Minamoto no Yoritomo became Japan's first shogun after initiating the Kamakura era (1185–1333).

A closer look at the Goshobo's name tells a tale. When it was first built, the Goshobo was located next to Arima's then only bathhouse, and was initially called Yuchigaya—meaning the entrance to the bathhouse—but this was changed to *Gosho* (meaning "imperial") near the end of the 1300s in honor of a visit from shogun Ashikaga Yoshimitsu. The *bo* (meaning "temple lodge") was then added some hundred years or so later to commemorate another venerable guest, Rennyo Shonin, the head-priest of Hongwanji Temple in Kyoto and the man who restored the Jodo Shinshu sect of Buddhism, which today is the most widely practiced branch of Buddhism in Japan.

Structurally, today the Goshobo largely dates to the early 1900s and has three types

of rooms, Tenraku (deluxe), Chuyo (superior), and Chikyu (standard). The modest Chikyu rooms, unusually for a ryokan, can be booked without meals, while the Tenraku and Chuyo offer a more traditional ryokan experience, with breakfast part of the plan.

The eight Tenraku rooms—the largest of the Goshobo's rooms—were built in the 1920s and beyond the combination of paper screens, tatami, and other classic ryokan design elements each exhibit the work of a novelist or poet associated with the ryokan. There are letters and books by the novelist Junichiro Tanizaki, who wrote about the Goshobo in his novel *A Cat, A Man, and Two Women* and, a must-read for anyone interested in Japanese design, wrote the definitive essay on Japanese aesthetics, *In Praise of Shadows*. There are also writings by the samurai and former prime minister, Hirobumi Ito, as well as historian and novelist Eiji Yoshikawa, who wrote about the sound of trickling water one can

hot-spring baths, the Kongosen and Shihoan. The latter, open air and candle lit—and serenaded by the hypnotic tinkling melody of a sixteenth-century *suikinkutsu* (an underground chamber into which water drips and echoes)—looks out on a lush garden, while the former is semi open-air and features distinctive iron-orange water.

Tosen Goshobo 陶湶 御所坊

Address: 858 Arima-cho, Kita-ku, Kobe 651-1408
Telephone: 078-904-0551
Website: http://goshoboh.com
Email: Via an online form
Number of rooms: 20
Room rate: ¥¥¥¥

Above Book one of the eight highest-end rooms—the Tenraku—and you have exclusive access to a bathhouse gently scented by the wooden interiors and with views out onto a pretty garden.

hear from some rooms. Guests in Tenraku rooms also have access to the private Shihoan area, with an open-air bath as well as a Zen garden and tea-ceremony room.

The three Chuyo rooms date to the 1950s and have what the Goshobo calls a "neo-Japanesque atmosphere", either offering views of the Goshobo's Zen garden and the verdant Mount Rokko mountains or overlooking the Taki River.

Food here is traditional *Yamaga-ryori*, a "polished rustic" style of cuisine—delivered in a special dining area with

kaiseki aplomb—for which the Goshobo sources some of the finest local ingredients: Kobe beef and Tajima beef, seafood such as Matsuba crab and firefly squid from the Seto Inland Sea, and organic rice, vegetables, herbs, and sake produced on its own farm.

When it comes to bath time, the Goshobo is in one of Japan's most renowned hot-spring areas. Mentioned in the sixth-century *Nihon Shoki* (Chronicles of Japan), legend has it that the Arima Onsen was discovered when the Shinto gods Onamuchi-no-Mikoto and Sukunahikona-no-Mikoto witnessed three injured crows healing themselves in the mineral-rich waters. However it may have come to attention, the result at the Goshobo is a pair of charming natural

A blast from the past. Many ryokan will collect guests from the nearest station (some have set daily pick-up times, others will come if you call), but the Tosen does it with retro style in a vintage bus.

Few ryokan can match the Sekitei when it comes to the garden and the views. Overlooking Hiroshima Bay and with traditional landscaping visible from each of the spacious villas, it's become known as one of the most attractive ryokan in western Japan.

On the side of a hill overlooking Hiroshima Bay and the small island of Miyajima, with an ornate garden that hugs the sloping hillside and a small selection of peaceful, traditionally appointed rooms, the Sekitei stands out as one of western Japan's premier ryokan for good reason.

The garden, built along with the rest of the Sekitei in 1965, is considered one of the Sekitei's star attractions—the ryokan is sometimes referred to as "Garden Inn Sekitei"—centered around a large pond accented by large rocks, shrubs, and miniature pines, borrowing the scenery (as many classic Japanese gardens do) of Hiroshima Bay and Miyajima as its backdrop and transforming its colors with the seasons—whether that's the pink and white blossoms followed by purple wisteria of spring or the varied shades of green that take over in summer.

Being so close to the bay, seafood obviously plays a key part at dinner time. The Hiroshima area is famed for its oysters, which depending on the day might make it into the *kaiseki* alongside local crab, shrimp, and Miyajima's signature dish, *anago meshi*—sea eel grilled with a sweet-soy basting and then chopped and popped on top of a bowl of rice. Both dinner and breakfast are served in-room, which means dining in one of the ten detached villas that, partially encircling the garden, look out onto landscaping and then down to the bay.

The villas themselves have a 1960s retro charm to them in places. Although at heart they share many classic ryokan

Above The garden at the Sekitei isn't just for looking at, its pathways are perfect for a scenic stroll.
Above right Design-wise, the Sekitei's villas are certainly distinctive. They have many traditional elements, but also a unique usage of such things as stone and rock that give an almost Mediterranean feel—not to mention a welcoming lack of uniformity.

design components, there's a deliberate and defining lack of uniformity. There are tables of different shapes and sizes, and touches like low leather couches or wooden rocking chairs looking toward the garden through wide windows and open terraces. Seven of the villas have their own private hot-spring baths, too, featuring aromatic cedar tubs in wood-decked semi open-air spaces—alternatively, there are modest, gender-separated indoor and outdoor communal baths.

As a base, the Sekitei is in a prime position for taking in one of Japan's most iconic sights, the "floating" *torii* gateway at Itsukushima Shrine on Miyajima island, which is a ten-minute ferry trip from the mainland, across the narrow Onoseto

Strait. Fifty-five feet (seventeen meters) in height, the *torii* was first put here in 1168, some five hundred years after the shrine was originally said to have been built, and the current incarnation, which appears to float when the tide is in, dates to the 1870s.

A little further away, one can also easily visit Hiroshima, a city indelibly linked with tragedy, but nonetheless another must-visit. As the site of the world's first atomic bombing, which occurred on the morning of August 6, 1945, in an instant killing some 80,000 (and over time claiming 60,000 more), Hiroshima's skeletal Gembaku Dome, Peace Memorial Park, and Peace Museum have become potent and in places harrowing symbols of the horrors of nuclear war.

Sekitei Inn 石亭
Address: 3-5-27 Miyahama-onsen, Oono-cho, Hatsukaichi, Hiroshima 739-0454
Telephone: 0829-55-0601
Website: www.sekitei.to
Email: info@sekitei.to
Number of rooms: 10
Room rate: ¥¥¥¥

Above Privacy is a key feature at the Sekitei, and that stretches to dining, with both meals served in-room, which means dinner with views of Hiroshima Bay, where some of the seasonal seafood served is sourced from.
Left Most of the villas have open-air baths that allow guests to enjoy a private soak in natural hot-spring water, but for hot-spring aficionados there is also a selection of indoor and outdoor communal baths to choose from.

Traditional architecture comes in many styles in Japan. The Sansou Murata celebrates that diversity with a collection of historic structures brought together from far and wide and transformed into a quaint retreat from the stresses of modern living.

A staff member greeting guests, not in a formal kimono or *yukata*, but in traditional form of dress that's far more comfortable, the *samue*, originally working clothes worn by monks.

Among the building styles is this thatched Meiji era cottage. Beyond being an atmospheric place to stay, this like many of the cottages and villas is also large—big enough for whole or even extended families, which isn't often the case at normal hotels or even many ryokan in Japan.

Thatched villas set against a mountainous backdrop. Kawara roof-tiled cottages enshrouded by forest. But for the sounds of nature—the summer shrill of cicada, the creaking of timber as spring breezes rock the trees— silence. The small collection of buildings that make up the Sansou Murata offer a retreat of calm and relaxation.

Situated at the foot of Mount Yufu on the outskirts of Yufuin Onsen, a hot-spring area in Oita Prefecture in Kyushu, the Murata appears as if it has been nestled among the ancient trees here for centuries. It might be a surprise, then, that it's a

relatively new addition. The twelve detached guesthouses and the main ryokan building, all more than one hundred years old, were only moved here from Niigata Prefecture (more than six hundred miles [nearly one thousand kilometers] away) in 1992.

Peek inside and the bucolic surrounds give way to a smart blend of traditional and contemporary, rural and urban. The thatched Meiji villa, for example, combines five bedrooms—two tatami matted, three with rustic dark woods and Western-style beds—with a large lounge area full of leather couches and a "fireside room" in the center of which comes an open *irori* hearth. In the Kichi cottage, the mix of ingredients is similar; one room is tatami, one earthen-floored, others wood-floored, and the aged woods are countered with retro Scandinavian furniture and abstract art on the walls. Like all the villas and cottages, both have their own hot-spring baths, too.

Wander around the grounds and you find a collection of facilities that are unusual for a ryokan. There is a bright and airy contemporary art gallery (Artegio) and a Meiji-era (1868–1912) house with log fire and cavernous beamed ceiling that's been transformed into a low-lit bar and lounge (Tan's Bar). There's a very sleekly designed chocolatier and tea house (Theo Murata), a patisserie specializing in Swiss rolls (B-Speak), and a soba-noodle restaurant, too. Although, when eating is concerned, dinner is the undoubted winner here.

Utilizing local produce and seafood, the evening *kaiseki* course is served in room and runs through a traditional line-up of courses, from seasonal appetizer

Left The main building has a very homely atmosphere, what with the scent of the wood fire and the warmth of the wooded interiors.

Below Tan's Bar. By day Tan's opens to the public as a café, but from 6pm until it closes at 11pm, it becomes a quieter spot for a nightcap for guests only.

and then sashimi selection through to locally raised chicken or beef that could be grilled, fried, or in a hot pot for the main course. Breakfast, which is taken in private spaces in the main building, can either be a traditional Japanese affair of rice, grilled fish, and other trappings, or a continental breakfast if you prefer.

Moving away from the Murata, the Yufuin area itself is a pleasant area to explore, quieter and more laidback than the far more famous Beppu hot-spring area (and its bubbling pools) sixteen miles (twenty-six kilometers) away. Easily accessed from the ryokan, Lake Kinrinko, which unusually has both hot and cold springs bubbling from its depths, is especially pretty when fall comes, while any time of year Yufuin's selection of art

Left Mind your head. Or use the other door. You find some fascinating mixing of styles inside some cottages—with extremely rustic touches like an open hearth, plastered walls, and wood beams alongside far more modern leather couches.
Below It's not only the cottages that are varied in style. The antique furnishings have also been carefully curated.

galleries and museums is always worth exploring, whether that's the Yufuin Yume Art Museum and its collection of painting and photography by wandering artists Kiyoshi Yamashita, the Hiroshi Hara-designed Sueda Art Museum and its work by contemporary sculptor Ryusuke Sueda, or the folk crafts (and demonstrations) like indigo-dying, *washi* paper-making, and pottery at the Folk Craft Village.

Sansou Murata 山荘 無量塔
Address: 1264-2 Kawakami, Yufuin-cho, Oita 879-5102
Telephone: 0977-84-5000
Website: www.sansou-murata.com
Email: murata@sansou-murata.com
Number of rooms: 12
Room rate: ¥¥¥¥

Left The private bath in the Tou cottage has a very unique design. This cottage is one of the more Western in style, with beds and a carpeted lounge, although it does have one tatami room.

Below The Higashi villa, which can sleep four, is one of the more traditional in style.

With just five villas immersed in an expanse of nature, the Tenku-no-Mori gives a sense of seclusion from not just other guests, but from the rest of the world.

The Tenku-no-Mori, a self-described "desert island in the macrocosm" spread over 148 acres (sixty hectares) of lush mountain forest in Kagoshima Prefecture, is about as exclusive as accommodation in Japan gets. There are only five villas here, all so detached from each other that guests can feel entirely removed from the world beyond, and they come at the kind of price that even by the standards set by many of the high-end properties in this book, sets them far apart (up to ¥200,000 per person per night!)

Of those five villas, three are for staying guests and two are for day-use only—the latter for a brief retreat with a lot of spa pampering and picnicking in sheer peace and quiet—but they all share certain characteristics that make them both extremely chic and yet naturally blended into their surrounds. Spacious and open-planned, they are defined by exposed wood beams and floor-to-ceiling windows that afford panoramic views across the Kirishima mountain range, and all come with vast wood-decked areas that cup open-air natural hot-spring baths to be enjoyed without disturbance, perhaps with champagne chilling in an ice-filled bucket on the terrace for some bath-time refreshment.

As well as the baths, around the Tenku-no-Mori there are a succession of other places to unwind. Guests could take in the views from a swing hanging from a tree. Maybe chill out by the river that runs

property to take in the sights of Kagoshima by air, in the process hovering near the volcanic Mount Sakurajima for the rarest of views, or to drop them off for a connecting flight at Kagoshima Airport. Cessna charters are possible, too. Less expensive, but no less special for guests in need of extra pampering, is a wide range of massage and beauty treatments, while private training, yoga, or meditation sessions can also be arranged.

As for the local sights beyond the Tenku-no-Mori, about a mile (about two kilometers) away is another property run by the same family, Gajoen (www.gajoen.jp), a far more affordable and rustic affair than Tenku-no-Mori but one that could easily have been included in this book in its own right. Between the two are several worthwhile places to visit, including the

through the complex, watching a kingfisher flitting between rocks if you're lucky. Perhaps relax on the decking that overlooks the Tenku-no-Mori's terraced farm, which produces the majority of the fully organic produce used by the resort's chefs. Food, included in the price, relies heavily on the more than thirty varieties of vegetables grown here, as well as on the prized chickens reared on the Tenku's free-range Wasure-no-Sato chicken farm. The food defies a simple definition; it's not pure *kaiseki* or pure European, it's simply natural, and it can be served al fresco or in-room.

Money seemingly being no object for the typical guest, the kind of activities Tenku-no-Mori differ from other resorts. Guests can book a helicopter ride from the

Above and left There's no shortage of space anywhere at the Tenku-no-Mori, whether that's the bedrooms, outdoor decking, or anywhere else where one might enjoy a moment of solitude: quite a rarity in Japan.

118-foot (36-meter) high Inukai waterfalls, rightly described by prominent (yet tragic) figure Sakamoto Ryoma as "a rare place possessing unbridled otherworldly beauty".

Ryoma played a key role in overthrowing the Tokugawa shogunate in the 1860s and bringing about the Meiji Restoration, although the tragic part of his tale is that he never got to see how the restoration would pan out. He was assassinated aged thirty-one in Kyoto in

Below The majority of the food served here comes from the Tenku's own on-site farm. Fully organic, it gives the chefs a wide range of in-season produce to work with. This part of Japan is also known for the quality of its chicken, and the Tenku has its own free-range poultry farm nearby.

1867, a year before the Meiji era commenced, but not before he helped broker peace between what are now Kagoshima Prefecture and Yamaguchi Prefecture, a local connection that isn't forgotten in these parts. There's even a hot-spring park nearby, complete with statue of him and his wife, that's been named after him.

Tenku-no-Mori 天空の森
Address: Minami-Kirishima Onsen, Syukukubota, Kirishima, Kagoshima 899-6507
Telephone: 0995-76-0777
Website: http://tenkunomori.net
Email: Via an online form
Number of rooms: 3
Room rate: ¥¥¥¥¥

Top Left Outdoor hot-spring baths at many ryokan snuggle up to buildings. At the Tenku they are smack bang in the open, where you can feel the breeze as you soak looking up at the stars.

Be it a bit of champagne on a comfortable reclining chair beside your outdoor bath (right), an afternoon in your hammock (above), a spa treatment, or an hour or two with a book by the river that flows through the property, the Tenku is all about relaxation and pampering.

Commanding views of Ishikari Bay and a combination of unique design features and equally unusual history make the Ginrinsou one of Hokkaido's most distinctive ryokan.

Above Certainly not a typical architectural element, Ginrinsou's tower, which guests can climb via several severely steep flights of wooden steps, was designed so the original owner could watch over his fleet in the bay.
Right Step up from the *genkan* area and you greeted by another unusual design feature—an inner dry landscaped garden that in keeping with Zen traditions employs raked sand and a careful positioning of rocks.

Perched above the port city of Otaru, with sweeping views out over Ishikari Bay, the Ginrinsou traces its roots to a different time, to when Otaru was (from modern eyes) an unlikely economic powerhouse—referred to as the Wall Street of the North—thanks to its role as a trading hub that connected Hokkaido not just to the rest of Japan but to the US, UK, and other parts of Asia, and especially for its thriving herring fisheries industry.

Built in 1873, Ginrinsou is one of Otaru's old "herring estates", the former residence of fisheries magnate Yasunojo Inomata, who like others made wealthy by the herring of Ishikari Bay, brought in master craftsmen from across Hokkaido to create a near palatial home. Originally located in nearby Yoichi (for whisky lovers, the home of Nikka Whisky's first distillery), over the course of a year it was relocated to its current hilltop perch in the 1930s, shortly after which it became a ryokan.

Inside, as you might expect for the former home of a multimillionaire, the "Herring House" (to use the Ginrinsou's nickname) is a charming and sprawling example of classic Japanese luxury. One that has some unique features, too. Climb the steep ladders of the distinctive watchtower that protrudes from the Ginrinsou's roof and you have a seagull's view of the entire bay—when located up the coast in Yoichi, one that allowed the owner to keep an eye on his fleet. Enter the lobby and you are met on one side by high-ceilings under which is a raked sand garden and the other by the tatami mats, hearth and screen paintings of the Ginrinsou's O-Hiroma meeting rooms. It's not hard to see why the Hokkaido government has designated Ginrinsou as one of its "one hundred most important cultural properties".

Then there are the guest rooms. They have bay views, and also feature all the classic ryokan ingredients—tatami, low table, paper-screen doors, calligraphy in

the *tokonoma* alcove, and futon put down at night. Some have in-room baths, too. If not, the Ginrinsou has excellent communal baths. In the mid-1980s, drilling work took place at the Ginrinsou to tap into natural hot-spring waters 4,000 feet (1,219 meters) below ground, enabling the ryokan to create outdoor baths of natural rock and marble that provide a panoramic view—particularly attractive as the sun sets into the bay.

Hokkaido is the breadbasket of Japan, known for its high-quality seafood—crab, shrimp, scallops, salmon roe, sea urchin, and more—as well as its beef brands and produce that ranges from multiple potato varieties to corn and melon. The *kaiseki*

Above Guest rooms come with views out to the bay and are just as attractive inside.

Right *Kaiseki* in Hokkaido means feasting on some of Japan's finest produce and seafood. The chefs at the Ginrinsou use Hokkaido's most well-known in-season items, which include a range of crabs and fish as well as farm-fresh melon, corn, potato, and more.

Right The *rotemburo* (outdoor hot spring) was a later addition at the Ginrinsou, a process that involved drilling deep into the earth to tap into a natural hot-spring source. The views from the water are stunning, especially at sunset and dawn.
Below In the small lounge area en route to the rooms, you find exquisite traditional art. Quite differently, you'll also come across a collection of Hokkaido wildlife—stuffed.

dinner at the Ginrinsou, served in-room or in the attached Ginrinsou Grill dining rooms, incorporates it all (herring included), although guests can opt instead for a multi-course French dinner.

Explore Otaru and you can find other local flavors to sample. Down by the popular Otaru Canal, lined by attractive nineteenth and early twentieth century stone buildings that recall Otaru's heyday, are places selling distinctly Hokkaido-style ice cream flavors (from lavender to sea urchin) as well as the local craft brewery, Otaru Beer, which brews a range of German-style beers. You could even make the thirty-minute train trip to Sapporo (see page 193 for more on Sapporo), Hokkaido's main city, for some of its signature northern dishes—mutton barbecue, miso ramen, and spicy soup curry.

Girinsou 銀鱗荘
Address: 1-1 Sakura, Otaru, Hokkaido 047-0156
Telephone: 0134-54-7010
Website: www.ginrinsou.com
Email: info@ginrinsou.com
Number of rooms: 14
Room rate: ¥¥¥¥

Below and bottom Ocean motifs are prevalent throughout the Ginrinsou. You'll see seahorses here, herring there, all a nod to the original owner's status as a fishing magnate. Even the name, Ginrinsou, follows suit—it means "silver scale house".

Above and top An easy half-day trip from Otaru is Nikka Whisky's original distillery in Yoichi, founded by Masataka Taketsuru and his Scottish wife Rita, whom he met while visiting Scotland to learn about Scotch. You can sample and buy some whisky here exclusive to Yoichi, but arguably the best thing is the smell. The vats here are in still in operation and they emit the sweetest aroma.

The Kuramure, a relatively new ryokan situated in a quiet corner of Otaru, offers a contemporary twist on the classic ryokan by combining sleek modern design elements with traditional hospitality.

Above Hokkaido is home to what many would say is the country's finest seafood, and ryokan in Otaru have access to the very best of it.
Below Each of the guest rooms is individually designed, giving the Kuramure a boutique hotel feel.

When it opened in 2002, the Kuramure added a very new dimension to Hokkaido's ryokan scene, with a blend of chic luxury and traditional minimal design that even fifteen years on makes it one of the most distinctive ryokan in northern Japan.

Like a boutique hotel, no two of the nineteen rooms here are exactly alike, but there is a unifying style in the uncluttered rooms featuring private hot-spring baths, understated wood flooring and tatami, a mix of traditional wallpapering and plastering, and sparingly placed furnishing inspired by Japanese and Chinese antiques. It gives the Kuramure a feeling that is contemporary, yet nostalgic; quite different to the ryokan norm.

Walk around the Kuramure and there are other signs that this is no ordinary ryokan. Serigraphs by local artist Tenei Abe decorate the halls. In places, windows at the base of walls let in shards of natural light, while revealing glimpses of the courtyard. Where rooms at ryokan often have names connected to nature, each room at the Kuramure is named after a writer, poet, or artist with a connection to Otaru. And in the library, guests can relax into sofas and armchairs with a selection of Japanese and English books, or select some vintage vinyl to play on the record player. There's also a sleek tea room, Furyuan, an ultra-contemporary space with white walls and white and sand-colored tatami that can be reserved so guests can enjoy their own private tea time.

Dinner at the Kuramure is based on *kaiseki*, with the head chef sourcing all ingredients from within Hokkaido and adding touches of contemporary and cosmopolitan verve to the fourteen-course meal—although it varies by season. Dishes might include sashimi of tuna belly, conger eel in a tomato jelly with parsley sauce, black wagyu beef with foie gras, and locally caught sea urchin. Breakfast is centered around Hokkaido rice, with pickled vegetables, grilled fish, and fruits among the line-up. Both meals are served in a private dining room—with a choice of table seating or sunken *horigotatsu* seating—away from the guest room (as the ryokan explains) to keep any odors from lingering.

Left The outer stone walls encased in wire are one of the outstanding design elements of the Kuramure, although so too is the use of ceramics, antiques and other accents to decorate the otherwise often minimalist interiors.

Below The cobbled streets and old warehouses of the Otaru Canal hark back to the town's time as a thriving commercial and fishing hub. Now filled with craft shops, restaurants, and bars, the old warehouses are well worth a visit, even if it's just to enjoy the way they reflect onto the canal.

One traditional facet of the Kuramure are the communal baths, set inside and outdoors, within earshot of the babbling of the Asari River and in sight of the Kuramure's natural-looking garden, which will be covered in snow in Hokkaido's long winter, but then full of seasonal colors in spring, summer, and fall.

Away from the ryokan, guests can easily explore Otaru (see more on Otaru on page 188) or visit Sapporo, Hokkaido's main city, which is only twenty miles (thirty-two kilometers) away and connected with frequent train services. Sapporo's Odori Koen, a belt of green park that runs through the city's heart, is home to an acclaimed jazz festival in summer, while in February it is the main site of the Sapporo Snow Festival, which attracts two million visitors with its giant snow and ice sculptures. Beyond that there are many historic sights and old Western-style buildings dating to Hokkaido's initial Japanese settlement some 150 years ago, as well as a pretty botanical garden that also houses a museum for learning about Hokkaido's indigenous Ainu people. And, of course, there's the food—Sapporo (like Otaru) has some of Japan's freshest seafood, plus hearty regional specialties such as miso ramen, soup curry (like mulligatawny) and a style of mutton barbecue named after Genghis Khan. If you can drag yourself away from the calm of the Kuramure, it's well worth the day trip.

Kuramure 蔵群
Address: 2-685 Arisagawa Onsen, Otaru, Hokkaido 047-0154
Telephone: 0134-51-5151
Website: www.kuramure.com
Email: Via an online form
Number of rooms: 19
Room rate: ¥¥¥¥

ZABORIN NISEKO

Another relative newcomer, the Zaborin is the epitome of a contemporary ryokan, fusing traditional cuisine, design elements, and *omotenashi* (hospitality) with a laid-back, mature hipness, and connectivity to nature.

wide windows that open out onto pastoral views of Hokkaido.

As a highlight, each villa also boasts both private indoor and outdoor hot-spring baths, using mineral-rich water sourced from half a mile (about a kilometer) below ground that arrives at ideal bathing temperature—hot enough to soothe and relax, but not too hot that one can't enjoy a long soak. The outdoor baths in particular allow one to immerse oneself

Below An appreciation of nature and a desire to have guests connect with it are key concepts at the Zaborin. At each and every turn, one catches glimpses of the natural world—shards of light breaking into a hallway or shimmering reflections of the woods on the windows. It's the kind of place where you are rewarded with magical moments when you slow down and take the time to ponder your surroundings. You can't help but unwind.

Sometimes, the kanji (Chinese characters) used in a ryokan's name go straight to the essence of the place. Zaborin is no exception. Nestled in the tranquility of a private forest in the Hanazono area of Niseko, Zaborin—comprising *zabo* (to sit, to forget) and *rin* (a wood)—is a merging of Japanese tradition and contemporary comfort designed to allow guests to forget the outside, to meditate, and to reconnect with oneself and with nature.

Opened in 2015, the Zaborin is by far the newest of the ryokan in this book, but that's certainly no bad thing. Starting with a blank slate has allowed the Zaborin free rein to combine the finest elements of a traditional ryokan with those of a contemporary hotel. Each of the fifteen villas is a spacious blend of east and west, featuring couches and modern amenities like flat-screen TVs, accents such as black-and-white photography of the local area, a (depending on the villa) varying mix of wood flooring and tatami (of Western-style beds and futon, too), and

in both the healing waters and nature, with views into the calm tranquility of the Hanazono woods.

Under head chef Yoshihiro Seno, a Hokkaido native who has worked at Japanese fine dining restaurants in Tokyo and New York, the Zaborin offers *kaiseki* with a distinctly earthy, natural Hokkaido feel. Served in private dining spaces, and arriving on a fashionably rustic mishmash of ceramic dishes and wooden trays and

Above There are no communal baths at the Zaborin, but it doesn't need them because each villa enjoys both an indoor and outdoor bath—some made of aromatic woods, some made of stone—for a fully private soak in natural hot-spring water. **Right** Chef Yoshihiro Seno creates works of art with many of his dishes. This one, featuring seasonal, locally sourced organic vegetables, he designed to resemble a half of Mount Yotei during a full moon.

Above Hokkaido being Hokkaido, Chef Seno doesn't only serve great vegetables, he has access to high-quality seafood (served here as a sashimi platter) and meats.

Right The outdoor baths look out into the woods. Soak for a while and the silence will occasionally be punctuated by the sounds of wildlife, which from time to time will also come into view.

Below right It's beds not futon in the villas, but in keeping with the overall ambience they are incorporated into a spacious, uncluttered style that, while contemporary, reaches deep into classic Japanese design sensibilities.

boxes, Zaborin's *kita-kaiseki* (or northern *kaiseki*) incorporates many of the flavors that make Hokkaido a major destination for foodies. The menu varies by season and availability, but expect the multi-course feast to include an assortment of fresh sashimi—perhaps with Hokkaido scallops and local crab—local mountain vegetables, Hokkaido-raised wagyu beef, and other fare artistically presented by chef Seno.

After dinner—or any time—the Zaborin has numerous corners in which to relax. There's a library with a collection of design books, and a lounge punctuated by

Left You'll find objets d'art carefully placed throughout the communal areas of the Zaborin, ranging from sculptures like this to artistic use of simple items like dead wood.

Below Built low to the ground, the Zaborin blends into the surrounding birch forest.
Bottom With a smoldering fireplace and views into the woods, the lounge and library is a beautiful, calming spot for a coffee or something stronger.

the crackle and aroma of an open fire. There's a low-lit counter bar for a nightcap and the Chanoza alcove for taking green tea with traditional sweets. There's a massage room too, offering shiatsu, oil, and sports massages—something you might want after a day skiing.

That each of the villas has been assigned a crest representing a different type of snow tells you something of the local environment. Niseko is Japan's premier winter sports destination, blessed with high-quality powder snow and a collection of interconnected ski resorts on the 4,291-foot (1,308-meter) Mount Niseko-Annupuri, which from late November to early May has runs that cater to all levels and ages of skiers and snowboarders, with striking view of the near-symmetrical peak of Niseko's other major mountain, the 6,227-foot (1,898-meter) Mount Yotei. Outside of ski season, Niseko draws visitors with its natural beauty—flower-carpeted fields, rugged peaks, and rolling farmland—hot springs, and a range of non-winter sports. And year round, it now has a place to sit and to forget.

Zaborin 坐忘林
Address: 76-4 Hanazono, Kutchan, Abuta District, Hokkaido 044-0084
Telephone: 0136-23-0003
Website: http://zaborin.com/en
Email: info@zaborin.com
Number of rooms: 15
Room rate: ¥¥¥¥

HINA-NO-ZA LAKE AKAN

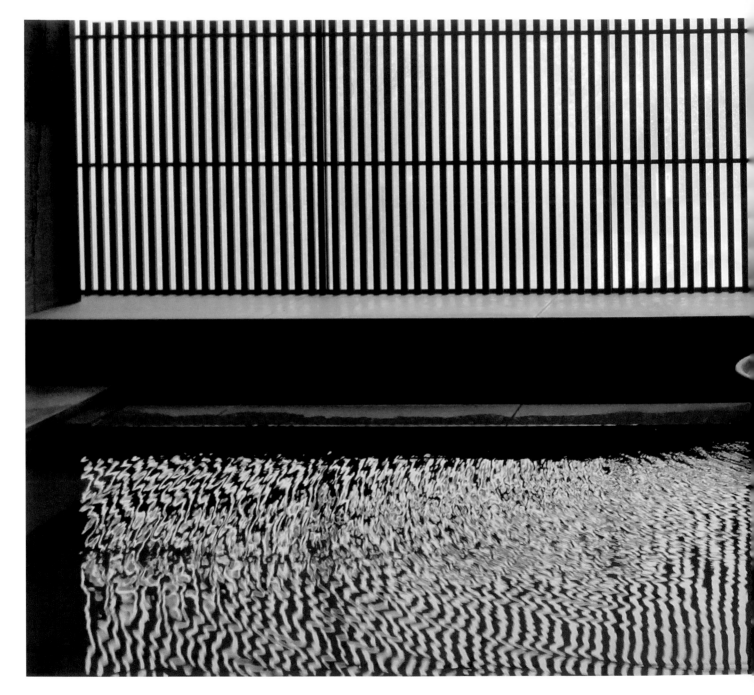

Beautiful to look at and surrounded by beauty too, the Hina-no-Za is a peaceful retreat in one of the most scenic parts of Hokkaido.

On the shores of the majestic Lake Akan, the Hina-no-Za boasts a wonderful natural setting that changes dramatically with the seasons, from the earthy colors of fall and carpeting of snow in winter through to lush green and clear blue skies in the mild summer.

Shaped by volcanic activity more than six thousand years ago, Lake Akan in eastern Hokkaido is known as one of Japan's most attractive and diverse caldera lakes, its clear waters and densely wooded surrounds home to an incredible range of flora, fauna, and wildlife, from peculiar *marimo* algae balls to majestic Blakiston's fish owls. Nature lovers in need of some ryokan pampering couldn't choose a better setting than here at the Hina-no-Za.

There are five room categories at the Hina-no-Za, with twenty-five suite-size rooms in all, although no two rooms look exactly alike. The Ama-no-Za suites, for example, come with a tatami-mat room, a living room with sofa, a separate bedroom, and a private open-air bathtub made of Japanese cypress, plus winning views of Lake Akan. Umi-no-Za suites feature wood decking that extends from the living room to a private bath overlooking the lake. The Kaze-no-Za suites, which also have commanding lake views, are much more traditional in feel, with tatami, paper screen doors, and a room that includes a sunken *irori* hearth. Similar in style are the second-floor Kasumi-no-Za suites, which have their own terraces, and the Mori-no-Za suites, which unlike the other suites offer picturesque mountain views.

While each room has its own bath, no ryokan would really be complete without a communal bath. The Hina-no-Za has two—the seventh-floor Kin-no-Yumi, where the large stone bath affords views of

Lake Akan and the surrounding mountains through oversized semi-open windows, and the sixth-floor Gin-no-Shizuku, where the invigorating heat of the hot-spring water is balanced by cool breezes coming across the lake.

Then comes dinner, which at Hina-no-Za is classic multi-course *kaiseki* focused on locally sourced seasonal ingredients— perhaps some Tokachi wagyu steak, a sashimi platter featuring Hokkai shrimp and Hokkaido sea urchin, and a white asparagus tofu topped in a cress jelly, to name just a few of the possibilities. For more local flavor, these can be paired with a range of Hokkaido-made sake or, alternatively, wines from around the world. Breakfast and dinner can either be taken in-room or in private tatami-mat dining rooms that feature teahouse-inspired interiors and the option of floor seating, sunken *horigatsu* seating, or conventional table and chairs.

As with the dining areas, in communal areas, Hina-no-Za balances contemporary with rustic, in the process honoring its natural surrounds. Most striking, the lobby features master carver Takeki Fujito's giant wood carving of a Blakiston's fish owl, which is regarded as a guardian by northern Japan's indigenous Ainu people.

Left Dinner draws on local flavors, in fall and winter incorporating into a traditional *kaiseki* course such things as hearty hot pots to fend off the cold.
Right Local woodcraft is a prominent feature throughout the ryokan, extending to the furniture.

In some places you can catch the gentle scent of fresh wood, in some areas you feel its smoothness underfoot. In other areas dark wooden beams and paneling give an aged counterpoint to modern furnishings, and then there are natural touches like the counter of the hotel's bar and lounge, which is made from a thirty-two-foot (ten-meter) long tree trunk—perfect for leaning on for an after-dinner cocktail or post-bath beer.

Hina-no-Za 鄙の座
Address: Akanko Onsen, Akanko, Kushiro, Hokkaido 085-0467
Telephone: 0154-67-5500
Website: www.hinanoza.com
Email: Via an online form
Number of rooms: 25 suites
Room rate: ¥¥¥¥

Top Hokkaido's indigenous Ainu people have a rich folk culture that goes back centuries—long before Hokkaido was settled by the Japanese. You can experience it through events like Ainu dancing at the Hina-no-Za. **Above** One of the bathing options with views out over the lake.

SARYO SOEN AKIU ONSEN, SENDAI

The combination of stunning (and vast) gardens and teahouse-inspired designs make the Saryo Soen well worth the bullet train fare north from Tokyo to Sendai. The ryokan may not be historic, but it's steeped in the finest ryokan traditions.

Some ryokan have modest stroll gardens on their grounds, others boast rooms with views of landscaped patches of green, Saryo Soen is very different. It's set in 6.4 acres (2.6 hectares) of traditional Japanese landscaping—replete with ponds and artfully arranged rocks, and colored a lush green in summer, earthy red and yellow in fall, white in winter, and with tints of cherry blossom pink in spring.

Built in 1991, but created with ryokan and teahouse traditions firmly in mind, at the Saryo Soen—which roughly translates as "garden teahouse"—the garden dominates. From the ten private villas, each of which has its own *rotemburo* (outdoor hot-spring bath), wide windows give a sense of being connected to nature. The other sixteen rooms, in the two-story main building, are also enshrouded in greenery,

When you have gardens as lovely as the Saryo Soen's, all you need is a comfy chair to relax into so you can take your time soaking it all up.

the first-floor rooms with decks that open onto landscaping and the second-floor rooms with an elevation that delivers sweeping garden views.

But the garden isn't everything. Another element that unites the rooms is the design, a mix of tradition and natural contemporary that sees tatami-mat and wooden flooring, wicker and wood furnishings, futon bedding in most rooms and villas, but Western beds in others.

One facet that remains firmly traditional, however, is the dining, with *kaiseki* menus that change monthly—beautifully presented on ceramic and lacquerware dishes, and with seasonal decorations such as maple leaves in the fall. The multi-course meals here might include shrimp and mushroom grilled in half-cut

One of the four communal baths at the Saryo Soen; this one looks onto its own dry landscaped garden.

Right One of the villas. The design is very traditional, yet its minimalist approach and use of natural tones also gives it a sleek contemporary feel.
Below Seasons play a major part of Japanese cuisine, and are reflected not just in the ingredients but in the presentation, with decorations such as fallen leaves in autumn, or ceramics featuring seasonal motifs.

eggplant, *ainame* (a kind of whitefish) blended into a patty with tofu and cooked in a light broth, or creatively prepared sashimi such as salmon roe served in fresh *yuzu* citron.

Bathing, too, is pure tradition. Located in the Akiu Onsen area, about nine miles (fourteen kilometers) west of central Sendai, the largest city in the Tohoku region, the Saryo Soen draws its waters from a mineral-rich hot-spring source, and as well as the in-room bathing boasts four communal baths, indoor and outdoor baths for men, and an indoor and outdoor baths for women. It also offers a range of spa and massage treatments.

The location also means it's easy to explore Sendai and its surrounding attractions, especially if you have a car. Sendai itself is a fairly modern city, but has historic attractions like the Zuihoden, mausoleum of legendary feudal lord Date Masamune, aka "the one-eyed dragon", who ruled the Sendai domain from 1600 to 1636. Other Sendai attractions include its take on the annual nationwide display of colorful streamers for the Tanabata festival (celebrating the celestial meeting of the deities Orihime and Hikoboshi; represented by the stars Vega and Altair) in early July, which Sendai combines with a major fireworks display, while to the north is the town of Matsushima and its strikingly beautiful bay. Ranked as one of the top three scenic sites in Japan (along with Miyajima and its "floating shrine" in Hiroshima Prefecture and the pine-tree covered sand bar of Amanohashidate in northern Kyoto Prefecture), the bay is dotted with tiny grey-rock islets that are accented by red and black pines, making it a very popular spot for boat trips.

Saryo Soen 茶寮宗園
Address: 1 Kamadohigashi-yumoto, Akiumachi, Taihaku-ku, Sendai, Miyagi 982-0241
Telephone: 022-398-2311
Website: www.saryou-souen.com
Email: souen@mitoya-group.co.jp
Number of rooms: 20
Room rate: ¥¥¥¥

In rural Akita Prefecture, the Tsuru-no-Yu is about as rustic as a ryokan comes, immersed in nature and celebrating local countryside traditions in both the way it looks and the way it operates.

The entrance to the Tsuru-no-Yu almost looks like the entrance to a shrine; it's quite unusual. You aren't entering anywhere sacred, but it does feel like you are stepping back into the past.

Located deep in the rural surrounds of the Nyuto Onsen area in Akita Prefecture, way up in the north of the Tohoku region, Tsuru-no-Yu arguably has the most rustic location of any ryokan in this book, situated at the foot of the almost 5,000-foot (1,500-meter) Mount Nyuto, enshrouded in woods that turn rust and yellow in the fall, are painted white in the north's long winters, and then burst into a dense green when the warmth returns.

Look back to the early Edo era (1603–1868) and there are records of the feudal lords of Akita treating themselves to baths at Tsuru-no-Yu, but they couldn't keep the soothing northern waters to themselves for long. Public bathing has been documented at Tsuru-no-Yu's hot-spring baths since the late 1600s, with

people taking to the waters to cure or soothe a variety of ailments. Animals, too, which is how Tsuru-no-Yu is said to have got its name—after an injured crane (*tsuru*) was seen generations ago bathing itself in the hot waters (*yu*) by a local hunter.

Nowadays, Tsuru-no-Yu has four hot-spring baths, three gender-separated baths for guests only, and a large, milky-watered outdoor bath open to the public. Unusually (nowadays at least), the outdoor public bath, which is surrounded by silvery pampas and dense woods, is *konyoku*—mixed gender—so it isn't for the shy, even though it is permitted for one to cover oneself with a towel (also unusual).

Tsuru-no-Yu has a collection of lodgings in all, providing thirty-four varying types of room, from simple tatami-mat rooms in modern(ish) buildings to atmospheric farmhouse-like accommodation, and all is incredibly well priced at around ¥10,000 per person including meals. The Yamano Yado annex bears the closest resemblance to a typical ryokan, with tatami-mat rooms, screen doors, and other traditional ryokan features mixed with rugged wood beams and sunken hearths (called *irori*) in some of the rooms, but it's the old main building that is by far the worthiest building of note; its thatched roof, dark aged woods and timbers, sunken hearths to both warm the rooms and cook on, providing an old countryside feel perfect for the natural surroundings. The food at Tsuru-no-Yu matches the rustic surrounds, too, with fare

Left There are a variety of rooms available, from very rustic to quite conventional, but irrespective of room type or rate, many come with views into the thick forest that surrounds the property.

Above From afar, you could be forgiven for mistaking the Tsuru-no-Yu as some kind of old-fashioned looking farmstead.

Below Depending on the room and accommodation plan, dinner can be cooked over and served around an open hearth, something you don't get at a typical ryokan.

such as regional *sansai* (mountain vegetable) dishes, hearty mountain yam hot pot, and trout cooked on sticks placed upright around the *irori* hearth.

Away from the hot-spring area, there's a range of other places to visit, although it helps to have a car. About six miles (ten kilometers) southwest is the scenic Lake Tazawa, an almost perfectly round caldera lake with striking blue waters, while another six miles beyond the lake is Kakunodate, a town often called the "little Kyoto" of Tohoku, where old samurai residences (called *bukeyashiki*) that date to the same early-Edo age of Tsuru-no-Yu give parts of the town a very old-world feel. There are skiing and snowboarding options nearby as well, most notably at the

Tazawako Ski Resort, which overlooks the lake and offers a range of terrain suitable for beginners and advanced skiers—and after a good workout there, there are very few things better than soaking in the outdoor bath at Tsuru-no-Yu, letting the piping hot water soothe your muscles as snow falls all around.

Tsuru-no-Yu 鶴の湯
Address: 50 Kokuyurin Sendatsuizawa, Tazawa-ko, Senboku, Akita 014-1204
Telephone: 0187-46-2139
Website: www.tsurunoyu.com
Email: Unlisted
Number of rooms: 34
Room rate: ¥

Right The older rooms are a delight. Not only are guests treated to elements such as painted screen doors, but also to in-room sunken hearths. Here you can see the long hook hanging from the ceiling that is used to hold utensils such as a large cooking pot or heavy iron kettle over the hearth.

Left The rural setting of Tsuru-no-yu offers excellent opportunities for walks in the forest along mountain streams amidst spectacular scenery—a real treat!

Above Mixed (nude) bathing isn't very common anymore, but in some rural areas it still survives. There are also male-only and female-only bathing options at the Tsuru-no-Yu, although one of the milky baths is still *konyoku* (mixed).

RYOKAN TRAVEL TIPS

Best time to go

There is no bad time to experience Japan, but some seasons are more beautiful and easier to deal with than others. Be aware that prices can spike during the Golden Week holidays (Apr 29–May 5), the summer season (mid-July to early Sep) and the New Year's holiday (approx. Dec 26 to Jan 4), and booking for these periods needs to be done months in advance for many of the best ryokan. If you struggle with heat, July to September can be hard, although in Hokkaido and mountainous areas there is some respite from the high heat and humidity of Tokyo and Kyoto. Thinking of nature, late March through to mid-April is the time to catch the wave of cherry blossoms that sweeps northward across the country every spring. After that, the new greens of May create some equally lovely views, while October and November have similarly pleasant blue skies and

warm temperatures to spring, but bring with them stunning autumnal colors.

Booking a ryokan

All of the ryokan covered in this book can be booked directly via their website or by email in English. With all of these, be aware that they can book out far in advance, especially in peak seasons such as the summer holidays, Golden Week, and over New Year's. To look for other ryokan across Japan, try Japan-based English-language booking sites like Japanican and Rakuten Travel or the homepage of the Japan Ryokan and Hotel Association (www.ryokan.or.jp).

Checking in and out

Checking in and out at a ryokan is essentially no different to any other hotel. If you arrive before the check-in time (usually 3pm), you will be able to leave your luggage at the ryokan until your room is available. Even so, it's good manners not to turn up and leave baggage during the check-out rush. Check-out is typically by 10am. Payment will be upon check out and credit card will be fine. Visa and Mastercard are accepted by almost all ryokan, as is JCB, but American Express isn't always accepted.

Electricity

The electrical current in eastern Japan, including Tokyo, is 100 volts, 50hz alternating current (AC). In western Japan,

including Kyoto, Nagoya and Osaka, it's 100 volts, 60hz AC. Japanese sockets take plugs with two flat pins, so you may need to bring an adaptor.

Meals at the ryokan

In most cases, breakfast and dinner are part of the package, although it is becoming more common to find ryokan (especially at the budget to mid-range) offering alternatives such as dinner and board only or breakfast and board only. Meal times are confirmed at or shortly after check-in and there isn't much flexibility with them (see page 19 to read why and get a fuller rundown of ryokan etiquette). If you have dietary restrictions, tell the ryokan before arriving, as they source most ingredients daily.

Money

The currency of Japan is the yen. The universal symbol is ¥ but in traditional settings like a ryokan it will often be written in Japanese kanji, 円, pronounced *en*. Bank notes come in denominations of

¥1,000, ¥2,000 (rarely seen), ¥5,000, and ¥10,000. Coins come in ¥1, ¥5, ¥10, ¥50, ¥100, and ¥500. Japan has a reputation as a cash society, but you can pay the ryokan bill with a card such as JCB, Visa or Mastercard. Many restaurants, bars, taxis, and shops in cities accept these, too, but in the countryside, it pays to travel with cash to be safe. Just to be sure, it is always advisable to check beforehand whether cards can be used. ATM at most post offices take foreign-issued bank cards, including those using Amex, Cirrus, Maestro, Mastercard, Plus, and Visa. Convenience store ATM are increasingly accepting overseas cards, too (Seven Bank at 7-Eleven especially). As of writing ¥110 is worth US$1.

Mobile phone and Internet access

You might find that you can use your own mobile phone in Japan if it has a roaming function, just be aware that fees can add up quickly. A much more economical option, if your phone is SIM-free, is to get a prepaid SIM card at the airport after landing. Depending on the airport, look for companies such as Mobal, B-Mobile, Japan Travel SIM, U-Mobile, and Ninja SIM, all of which offer decent deals on short-term SIM cards. Something else worth considering (especially as Japan lags on widespread public Internet connectivity, and ryokan are very often without Wi-Fi) is renting a portable Wi-Fi router to give you Internet access wherever you go. Again, this is best organized upon arrival at the airport, through major telecoms firms like Softbank and Docomo and smaller (but often with

better deals) companies such as Japan Wireless or Rental Wifi. Rates vary, but expect to pay around ¥3,000 to ¥5,000 for five or so days of unlimited data usage or ¥10,000 to ¥12,000 for a month.

Ryokan access

In cities such as Kyoto, access tends to be easy. Hop in a taxi and say the ryokan name and you'll be fine. Having the phone number handy for the driver to put into his car navigation system is a good back-up just in case there are communication issues. In hot-spring resort towns and rural areas, it can be a little harder. Some ryokan run free shuttles to and from the nearest station at set times. Some don't, so you might require a longer taxi ride. All the ryokan in this book have access information on their websites (see the relevant listings), so you can plan accordingly beforehand.

What's included in the fee?

The room and main meals will come as a package, but alcohol and soft drinks from the menu at meal times will be charged

separately (the tea is free). Likewise, anything in the in-room fridge is most likely charged separately unless someone tells you otherwise (there will be a menu on or by the fridge). Other than the welcome drink or self-serve tea, anything you drink or eat in lounge areas or in-hotel bars is typically charged separately, too. If you use the TV, some movie channels require paid access (this will be detailed on the screen). Access to the baths will be free for guests (and usually off-limits to non-guests), but some ryokan also have private baths that can be booked for a fee. Massage and spa services also cost extra, as would entertainment such as bringing in a private geisha. It depends on the ryokan, but payment for these generally occurs at check-out, so you don't need to carry cash around the ryokan (you just charge to your room). Room rates in the book are per person per night, unless otherwise stated.

¥ US$100~
¥¥¥ US$300~
¥¥¥¥ US$500~
¥¥¥¥¥ US$1,000~

Published by Tuttle Publishing, an imprint of
Periplus Editions (HK) Ltd.

www.tuttlepublishing.com

ISBN 978-4-8053-1392-3
Library of Congress Cataloging in Process

Distributed by
North America, Latin America & Europe
Tuttle Publishing
364 Innovation Drive, North Clarendon,
VT 05759-9436 U.S.A.
Tel: 1 (802) 773-8930; Fax: 1 (802) 773-6993
info@tuttlepublishing.com; www.tuttlepublishing.com

Japan
Tuttle Publishing
Yaekari Building, 3rd Floor,
5-4-12 Osaki, Shinagawa-ku, Tokyo 141-0032
Tel: (81) 3 5437-0171; Fax: (81) 3 5437-0755
sales@tuttle.co.jp; www.tuttle.co.jp

Asia Pacific
Berkeley Books Pte. Ltd
3 Kallang Sector #04-01, Singapore 349278
Tel: (65) 6741 2178; Fax: (65) 6741 2179
inquiries@periplus.com.sg; www.tuttlepublishing.com

22 21 20 19   10 9 8 7 6 5 4 3 2
Printed in Hong Kong   1907EP

ACKNOWLEDGMENTS

Akihiko (Alan) Seki wishes to thank Elizabeth Heilman Brooke, who made
a great contribution to his first "Ryokan" book as writer, and to Thomas
Daniell, who supported his "Kyoto" project as an architect-writer. He also
extends his heartiest appreciation to his wife Asako, who spent a great deal
of time helping with this book—attending photo shoots, acting as his
assistant, coordinator, and sometimes design supervisor.

Rob Goss would like to thank his co-author for inviting him on board
this project and for sharing his knowledge on the ways of the ryokan. The
journey has been an incredible learning experience. I hope readers will take
with them equally unforgettable memories from visiting the ryokan in this
book. More than anything, love and thanks go to his wife Yoko, son Arthur
and faithful kuroshiba Henry for putting up with his frequent travels and
(as ever) making home the best place to travel to.

Finally, both photographer and author would like to thank all the ryokan
and their staff for their warm hospitality and cooperation. Without the
generous access and time given by all, this book wouldn't have been possible.

ABOUT TUTTLE:
"BOOKS TO SPAN THE EAST AND WEST"

Our core mission at Tuttle Publishing is to create books which bring
people together one page at a time. Tuttle was founded in 1832 in the
small New England town of Rutland, Vermont (USA). Our fundamental
values remain as strong today as they were then—to publish best-in-class
books informing the English-speaking world about the countries and
peoples of Asia. The world has become a smaller place today and Asia's
economic, cultural and political influence has expanded, yet the need for
meaningful dialogue and information about this diverse region has never
been greater. Since 1948, Tuttle has been a leader in publishing books on
the cultures, arts, cuisines, languages and literatures of Asia. Our authors
and photographers have won numerous awards and Tuttle has published
thousands of books on subjects ranging from martial arts to paper crafts.
We welcome you to explore the wealth of information available on Asia at
www.tuttlepublishing.com.